158555

 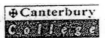

LEARNING RESOURCES CENTRE

To renew your books call us on 01227 811166 or online at
http://www.tinyurl.com/renew-my-book

Please return this book on or before the last date stamped below

0 8 JAN 2015		
2 2 APR 2020		
2 0 APR 2022		
1 7 APR 2024		

D1470693

Therapy in Practice

Series editor: Windy Dryden

Therapy in Practice is a series of books developed especially for therapists and students, which provides practical, accessible guidelines for dealing with clients with specific, but very common, problems. Books in this series have become recognised as classic texts in their field, and include:

Counselling for Alcohol Problems, Third Edition
Richard Velleman

Counselling Suicidal Clients
Andrew Reeves

Counselling for Grief and Bereavement, Second Edition
Geraldine M. Humphrey and David G. Zimpfer

Counselling and Psychotherapy for Depression, Third Edition
Paul Gilbert

Counselling for Post-Traumatic Stress Disorder, Third Edition
Michael J. Scott and Stephen G. Stradling

Counselling Survivors of Childhood Sexual Abuse, Third Edition
Claire Burke Draucker and Donna Martsolf

Career Counselling, Second Edition
Robert Nathan and Linda Hill

Counselling for Eating Disorders, Second Edition
Sara Gilbert

Counselling for Anxiety Problems, Second Edition
Diana Sanders and Frank Wills

Counselling for Stress Problems
Stephen Palmer and Windy Dryden

Therapy with Dreams and Nightmares

Theory, Research & Practice

Delia Cushway
and
Robyn Sewell

2nd
Edition

SAGE

Los Angeles | London | New Delhi
Singapore | Washington DC

Los Angeles | London | New Delhi
Singapore | Washington DC

SAGE Publications Ltd
1 Oliver's Yard
55 City Road
London EC1Y 1SP

SAGE Publications Inc.
2455 Teller Road
Thousand Oaks, California 91320

SAGE Publications India Pvt Ltd
B 1/I 1 Mohan Cooperative Industrial Area
Mathura Road
New Delhi 110 044

SAGE Publications Asia-Pacific Pte Ltd
3 Church Street
#10-04 Samsung Hub
Singapore 049483

Library of Congress Control Number: 2012936255

British Library Cataloguing in Publication data

A catalogue record for this book is available from
the British Library

Editor: Alice Oven
Assistant editor: Kate Wharton
Production editor: Rachel Burrows
Copyeditor: Solveig Gardner Servian
Proofreader: Derek Markham
Indexer: Elizabeth Ball
Marketing manager: Tamara Navaratnam
Cover design: Wendy Scott
Typeset by: C&M Digitals (P) Ltd, Chennai, India
Printed in India at Replika Press Pvt Ltd

ISBN 978-1-4462-4709-9
ISBN 978-1-4462-4710-5 (pbk)

To Colin for his loving personal support and professional encouragement

Contents

About the Authors

 **Delia Cushway** (BA, MSc Clinical Psychology, PhD, C Psychol clin/foren, ABPsS), is Emeritus Professor of Clinical Psychology at Coventry University and a practising Registered Clinical Psychologist. Delia worked for 20 years in clinical psychology training. Initially working at the University of Birmingham, she set up the Clinical Psychology Doctorate at the Universities of Coventry and Warwick in 1998 and was its Director until 2008. Before working as a clinical psychologist Delia worked in the Prison Service as a psychologist, where she served the equivalent of two life sentences before getting parole!

Delia grew up, psychologically speaking, at the same time as humanistic psychology and trained in the humanistic therapies of psychodrama, transactional analysis, and particularly Gestalt Therapy, in the 1970s. She has an integrationist clinical orientation with a strong humanistic philosophical base. Delia's research, teaching and clinical interests include dreamwork, reflective practice, supervision, Gestalt therapy, and stress and self-care, and she has written and published widely in these areas.

Delia discovered dreamworking through Gestalt therapy and started running dream groups when working with prisoners, whom she discovered often had rich and colourful dream lives. In 1985 she started running dream groups together with her friend and colleague Robyn Sewell, with whom she wrote the first edition of this book. Together they ran well over 100 dream workshops, including many at Vaughan College, for Leicester University's Adult Education programme, and at Westminster Pastoral Foundation, London. Delia's work with dreams and nightmares has continued to evolve, and she has incorporated more recent cognitive approaches into her clinical practice and workshops.

Robyn Sewell (BSc; Post Grad. Cert. in Ed; MSc Ed. Psychology; Dip. Group Psychotherapy; CPsychol AFBPsS)

After working for six years as a primary school teacher, Robyn joined H.M. Prison Service as a psychologist, and there she has spent most of her career.

After her formal retirement, she trained as Group Psychotherapist at the London Centre for Psychotherapy and then for some years she held a part-time lectureship on the Group Psychotherapy Course at Goldsmiths College London.

Her interest in dreams began back in the early 1980s, an interest she developed through talks and workshops in a variety of settings. Later, she linked up with Delia and together they ran many workshops, including a series of training workshops for Counsellors at Westminster Pastoral Foundation and at Leicester University's Adult Education Department.

She is now fully retired.

Foreword by Mark Blagrove

I read the 1992, 1st edition, of *Counselling with Dreams and Nightmares* and was intrigued by the case studies and possibilities outlined there, in the description of various dreamwork methods, for therapeutic and also personal growth. As an experimental psychologist I was very interested in the background theories to these methods, outlined so well in that book, and with the difficult question of how such claims of personal insight and growth could be investigated. I was very grateful to be able to discuss these issues with Delia Cushway over many years at the annual conferences of the International Association for the Study of Dreams. She, and that 1st edition, introduced me to a wealth of ideas and case study data that greatly expanded what I now see as having been a very narrow scientific approach to the content of dreams and nightmares, and to the study of the relationship between dreams and waking life.

Since 1992 the science of dreaming has expanded greatly, and that expansion is now described in this 2nd edition. At that time there was very little established knowledge about the functions of sleep, whereas since then the roles of the stages of sleep (REM, stage 2 sleep, slow wave sleep) in the consolidation of memories, and in the linking together of new with old memories, has become a major growth area in neuroscience. This research addresses how emotional events are laid down in memory, and also how trauma can be resolved, or can result in post-traumatic stress disorder. That dreams are reflective of the memory processing and consolidation that occurs during sleep is now a common assumption for many sleep researchers. This book addresses what may be the experiential side of that memory processing during sleep, and what can be done creatively with the dreams that result, and with our emotional reactions to those dreams.

The book covers the full range of dreams, from everyday dreams, lucid dreams (dreams where you know you are dreaming), ordinary nightmares, post-traumatic nightmares, and the arousal disorder of night terrors in children. The book will therefore be of interest to a wide range of readers, from those interested in what may be seen as their own ordinary dreams, to others who may have rarer types of dreams, such as nightmares and lucid dreams. It will also be of interest to counsellors and therapists who wish to respond to dreams that clients bring them.

Since 1992 there has been research on the way in which studying or appreciating dreams can be helpful to individuals, and research on the formation and treatment of nightmares. These advances are described in this edition. I know that a wide variety of people, whether as the professional or client in therapy or counselling, or as part of a personal appreciation and exploration of one's own dreams, or as part of a group that examines its members' dreams, will benefit from reading this book. Individuals working with more established counselling and therapeutic practices will also benefit from the links drawn between dreamwork and those methods. However, and quite rightly, the author also includes methods of looking at dreams that treat dreams as the starting point for a therapeutic or action-planning process, in which it is the activity that the dream inspires that can be beneficial, rather than the dream content itself.

This book integrates theoretical, experiential, clinical and research aspects of dreaming and of working with dreams. A knowledge of these four aspects is important for anyone interested in dreams, whether of their own dreams or those of others, whether professionally or as a lay interest, or even as a scientific interest. This expanded 2nd edition of what was a classic text is thus very welcome, and will inspire many people who are intrigued about why we dream, and what to do with our dreams.

Professor Mark Blagrove
Swansea University

Biographical note: Mark Blagrove is Head of the Department of Psychology and Director of the Sleep Laboratory at Swansea University, he is a past-President of the International Association for the Study of Dreams, and is a Consulting Editor for the academic journal *Dreaming*.

Preface and Acknowledgements

The first edition of this book was published 20 years ago. Since that time there have been significant developments in the field, and working with dreams and nightmares has become more accepted into mainstream cognitive therapeutic approaches. The increase of therapeutic work with trauma survivors has also necessitated the development of models for working with post-traumatic nightmares. However, I am surprised that so many colleagues working as psychological therapists still seem to be at a loss when presented with clients' dream material. Although I run workshops as requested, and on local clinical psychology training programmes, working with dreams and nightmares is still not regularly included on counselling and psychotherapy training courses. This is not the case in the USA where dreamwork and dreamwork education are much more widespread and are supported by the International Association for the Study of Dreams.

Much of the dream material included from the first edition was drawn from the workshops run by Robyn Sewell and myself at Vaughan College, Leicester and the Westminster Pastoral Foundation, London. Most of the new dream material in this edition is from my practice as a clinical psychologist and supervisor. Some colleagues have also generously contributed dream material. Names have been changed, as have some dream details to protect anonymity. Where people have specifically wished to be included, I have used their proper names and actual dreams. I would like to thank and acknowledge the contributions from the following people: Colin Bourn, Carol Butler, Ben Cushway, James Eyre, Maria Ferrins-Brown, Chris Gilbert, Annette Greenwood, Vicky Hoggard, Helen McGlasson and Mary McMurran. I would also like to thank the many workshop participants and clients whose dream material has enriched this book.

The book is intended to encourage and support psychological therapists of all orientations to work with their clients' dreams, as well as to stimulate their clients' interest in incorporating their dreams into waking life in their own way. It can also be used as a self-help guide for clients and for any dreamers who just want to understand their dreams. For some people the ability to manage and lessen the terror of their nightmares is paramount. Others just want to explore the richness and creativity of their dreams. However we want to use them, our dreams belong to us, the dreamers, and are available to us to interpret, to use creatively, to gain wisdom from, to play with or, if we choose, to ignore; it is up to us how we make sense of them.

Delia Cushway
March 2012

1

Introduction and Background to Dreamwork

Introduction and aims

In the 20 years since the publication of the first edition of this book there have been considerable developments in the field of dreaming, and it is timely to bring it up to date. When Robyn Sewell and I wrote our original book, working with dreams and nightmares was not common among psychological therapists. This may in part have been due to the psychoanalytic legacy of dream interpretation and to the gulf in understanding between behaviourist and analytic psychologists. The growth and development of cognitive therapies has opened the way for dreamwork to become more mainstream. In the last few years cognitive therapists have begun to be interested in dreams and are incorporating and adapting methods of dreamwork into the cognitive model.

In the last two decades working with trauma has also become very important. This has made the treatment of post-traumatic nightmares very salient and there have been new models developed, which need describing and outlining for the practitioner. Another therapeutic area which has been developed in this time is that of working with survivors of sexual abuse; working with nightmares is very important for this group. Until recently the systematic study of the dream experience was not thought to be a legitimate topic for scientific inquiry (Kramer, 2007) but with the introduction of cognitive approaches the science has moved forward and there is new evidence indicating that dreams may play an important role in information processing and memory consolidation.

This new edition will therefore be updated to take account of the developments outlined above. However, the main aim of this book has not changed. It is to describe the models and methods of working with dreams and nightmares so that they will be accessible to psychological therapists of all theoretical orientations, as well as to anyone who has a desire to work with their own dreams. While the book is intended as a practical guide, it is helpful to consider dreamwork in a historical perspective. The next section, therefore, briefly describes the history of dreamwork. It is also important for those working with dreams to have a basic understanding of the process of sleep and dreaming. Thus, in the final section of the chapter, dream interpretation will be set in the context of what is known from sleep and dreaming research.

Historical perspective

Ancient civilizations

Dreamwork and dream theories have an ancient and rich history with religious, spiritual and paranormal links. In ancient times dreams were seen as messages from the gods to warn, prophesy and encourage. Some of the earliest recorded information about dreams comes from the ancient Egyptians, who saw dreams as devices of the gods to communicate helpful information to mankind. There were basically two prescientific ways of interpreting dreams. The first method was to take the content of the dream as a whole and to interpret its meaning in another context. An example given by Freud and cited by Ullman and Zimmerman (1983) is the Old Testament story of Joseph dreaming that his brothers' sheaves of corn bowed down before Joseph's sheaf. The brothers took this as a sign that one day Joseph would be king over them. The second method was to use a 'cipher', whereby every image in the dream was looked up in a dream book. The ancient Greeks also interpreted dreams as messages from the gods, particularly with healing functions. The ancient Greeks were not the only people to experience miraculous cures in dreams. The ancient Hebrews, Indians, Chinese, Japanese and Muslims all practiced dream incubation; this was a practice whereby people would pray and ask for God or the gods to send a message via a dream that would provide the answer to a problem or suggest the cure for an illness. Most religious theorists today would not regard dreams as literally expressing the voice of God. A less literal and more contemporary religious viewpoint is represented by the work of Sanford (1968), who believes that it is the creative element in dreams which is divine. He is more concerned with the divine at work in the human soul rather than with elaborate creedal formulations.

Even without the belief that dreams are literally messages from the gods, it is possible to learn a lot about creative dreaming from ancient dreamers, who used their dreams in special ways to gain answers to their questions or to obtain cures from sickness. In her book, *Creative Dreaming*, Garfield (1974) explains that it is not necessary to believe in a special god or go to a sacred place to employ dream incubation. She states that the main essentials are to find a place where you feel peaceful, clearly to formulate your intention for a desired dream and to relax your body, concentrating on and visualizing your desired dream. (More detailed instructions in dream incubation will be given later in this book.) Clearly, the element of self-suggestion is important and can be as powerful as external suggestions like hypnosis. So one important thing we can learn from the ancients is that it is possible to induce healthful images into our dreams. Changes in dreams may change our waking attitudes which, in turn, may well affect our emotional and even physical well-being.

Native Americans

Whilst there is not the space to document the countless cultural uses of dreams, it is useful to give some attention to certain Native American tribes which assigned special importance in their lives to dreams. The ways that Native American cultures used dreams varied: often dreams were a part of the religious systems and provided a way for the dreamer to contact supernatural spirits and gain power from them. In consequence, dreams were also often a part of the social system, with a special status and role assigned to the dream interpreter. Dreams were almost universally used to predict the future, with rituals to get rid of bad dreams or to encourage good ones. They were sometimes used to manage psychological problems, a kind of early psychotherapy, in which dreams revealed wishes or indicated that certain rituals should be applied. Garfield (1974) documents these ideas more fully and suggests that we can learn from the Native Americans that, if we regard our dreams as important in our lives, we will receive and remember valuable dreams. She also suggests that our dreams will become more relevant to waking life if they are valued and used. Another important Native American concept is that of the value of obtaining 'dream friends'. The Native Americans encouraged offers of friendship in dreams from 'spirit guardians'. Garfield suggests that all friendly gestures in dreams should be accepted and appreciated. In the Senoi culture, which has been described by Garfield as well as Stewart (1969), dream interpretation represented the focal activity of day-to-day living. According to these writers, the Senoi, a tribe living in Malaysia, have achieved a high degree of internal and interpersonal integration on the basis of the communal analysis of dreams. They have pioneered and developed this as a method of psychosocial exploration. More reference will be made later in the book to Senoi techniques and their ways of working with nightmares.

Medieval religion

The coming of Christianity did not significantly alter ancient dream theories until around 300–400 AD, when Jerome, a church father and a contemporary of Augustine, had particularly tortured and troubled dreams and warned against false dreams and the possibility of demonic influence. Dreams then became associated almost exclusively with witchcraft, and those who paid attention to them were regarded as superstitious. Dream theories did not undergo much development through the following centuries, since the belief was encouraged that dreams were not from God and must be ignored. This view was strongly reinforced by the medieval Church, which was the dominant authority on thought and behaviour. The word of God had been given to the Church and ordinary people did not need God to speak to them through dreams; those who made such claims were viewed suspiciously or condemned. Certainly, it appears that wise people would not have talked about their dreams in the Middle Ages. Rycroft discussed reasons for this devaluation of dreams and considers that it was only within the twentieth century 'that dreams have aroused serious scientific interest and have been regarded as being as deserving of investigation as the shared objective world we perceive when awake' (1981: 1). He argued that prior to this time dreams, as subjective phenomena, were regarded as inherently resistant to the scientific method, at least as generally understood.

Twentieth and twenty-first century dreamwork

All modern dreamworkers consider that Freud's work, *The Interpretation of Dreams* (1900, reprinted 1976), marks a crucial turning point in the history of the study of dreams. In the next chapter there will be an outline of his theory, as well as descriptions of other psychological theories that have been influential in developing contemporary approaches. These are the theories of Jung, Fritz Perls and Ann Faraday.

Since the 1980s there has been a proliferation of popular dream books. Many of these books attempted to provide guides and hints for do-it-yourself dreamwork and did not regard interpretation as the sole right of the expert. Most of these approaches, however, rely on reworking the main theories listed above. There have been important dream models developed in the USA from influential workers such as Weiss (1986), Hill (1996, 2004), Barrett (2004) and Krakow (e.g. 2004). Many of these methods of dreamworking have been collected together in *Cognitive Therapy and Dreams* (Rosner, Lyddon & Freeman, 2004), which is a broad collection of methods from those working both in traditional cognitive therapy as well as from 'those working at the intersection of cognitive therapy and experiential therapy' (p. 6). These writers comment that the increasingly integrationist perspective of cognitive therapy makes it possible to embrace dreamworking under its umbrella.

It is worth drawing attention to one further aspect of dreaming that has been the subject of much development in recent years. Although there has always been an interest in the spiritual and paranormal aspects of dreams, one aspect is particularly relevant to therapy. There has been much research demonstrating and validating the phenomenon of lucid dreaming. In lucid dreams people become aware they are dreaming while they actually are dreaming, and are then able to control their dreams by thought. This work was pioneered in Britain by Green (1968), developed in the USA by La Berge (1985) and was continued by Hearne (1990). Subjects have been found who are good at lucid dreaming, and experiments have been conducted showing how this level of awareness or consciousness can be incorporated into dreams. More recent work, reported by Hamzelou (2010), has used experiments with lucid dreams to try to work out how the brain produces two subjective states of consciousness: primary consciousness or dreaming, and secondary consciousness or wakefulness with its reflective awareness. In the therapeutic context lucid dreaming has particular uses in the management of nightmares and will be described in more detail later.

Research into sleep and dreaming

In order for us to understand our own dreams and to help those we counsel, it is helpful for us to have some basic knowledge about the process of dreaming. There are many myths and so much folklore has been built up around the subject that it is helpful to sort out what has been established by research and what is still unknown to us. For example, many people today believe that they never dream, that dreams happen in an instant, or that people only dream when they are troubled or have problems. In fact, research about sleep and dreaming developed in the 1950s and 1960s and, although physiological findings cannot explain the psychological reasons for dreaming, they do provide information that enables the modification and development of some of these theories. Thus physiological research into the dreaming process is an important complement to the psychology of dreams.

Rapid eye movement (REM) sleep was first noticed by Aserinsky and Kleitman (1953). These American researchers were studying sleep patterns in babies when they noted that, at times during sleep, the infants' eyes moved in unison rapidly and jerkily under closed lids. Later, REM sleep was identified as a distinct stage of sleep occurring in all humans and higher animals. The development of the electro-encephalograph (EEG) machine, a device for recording the electrical activity of the brain, and of the electro-oculograph (EOG), an instrument for recording eye movement during sleep, have enabled researchers to recognize five stages of sleep. These are stages 1 to 4 and a distinct REM stage, which occurs as the sleeper moves from the deeper level (4 or 3) into a lighter level (1). This fifth stage of REM sleep is now generally associated with dreaming, since subjects woken during REM sleep are mostly able to recall a distinct and vivid dream. Dream reports from non-REM sleep are much less frequent, are shorter, and the dreams reported tend to be less distinct and dramatic.

There is a controversy over whether there are differences between REM and non-REM dreams (Blagrove, 2009).

Although the amount of time we spend in the different stages of sleep varies a little between individuals, an adult spends about 25 per cent of his or her sleeping time in REM, totalling between one-and-a-half to two hours a night. During the night we move through the stages of sleep in cycles lasting about 90 minutes. There are four or five cycles of sleep a night, with the REM periods increasing in length from about 10 minutes in the first cycle to up to 45 minutes in the later cycles towards morning. This pattern is somewhat different for a new-born baby, who may sleep for 17 hours a day and will spend between 60 per cent to 80 per cent of that time in REM sleep. In old age the amount of time we spend in REM sleep drops to about 20 per cent of sleeping time. Even adults who have been blind since birth and who report no visual dreams do experience REM sleep. Thus we can conclude that, contrary to popular myth, everybody does dream. This can be demonstrated experimentally by inviting disbelievers into a sleep laboratory and awakening them during a period of REM sleep. When this happens, researchers have shown that dreams or dream fragments are almost always recorded.

Even though all of us dream, some of us have greater dream recall than others. While 14 per cent of people report dreaming every night and 6 per cent report never dreaming, most of us remember our dreams some of the time. Although being interested in your dreams means that you are more likely to recall them, many studies have failed to demonstrate any personality correlates of frequency of dream recall (Blagrove, 2007). Clearly, however, nobody remembers all, or even most, of their dreams. Thus people who claim to remember all of their dreams are also misinformed. We can, especially if we make an effort, remember some selected dreams. The dreams that patients take to their analysts, therefore, are a selected sample. Psychoanalytic theories may therefore be valid for some of our dreams, but do not provide a comprehensive theory for the totality of our dreaming. Since all the higher animals also have REM sleep and most pet owners need no convincing that their pets do dream, it is probable that dreaming, or at least the brain activity associated with REM sleep, serves a physiological purpose.

Experimental evidence has also exploded other myths about dreaming. For example, it is a myth that dreams occur in a flash. In experiments, the longer the preceding REM sleep period before awakening the participants, the more words these participants tended to use in recounting their dreams. Also, participants woken after REM sleep had begun were fairly accurate in estimating how much time had elapsed. Therefore it seems that dreams do occur in 'real' time. Various reports, usually of spraying water onto unsuspecting participants in REM sleep and then waking them up, have shown that external stimuli are incorporated into dream accounts. For example, many of us have had the experience of looking for the lavatory in dreams only to wake up with a full bladder. There are people who rarely remember dreaming in colour. However, most sleep studies indicate that we do generally dream in colour, but that this aspect of the dream tends to be quickly forgotten unless it is a particularly important feature of the dream.

Another notable aspect of REM sleep is that, if subjects are systematically deprived of it, by being woken up each time they go into REM sleep, the disturbing effects of sleep loss are manifested more rapidly. Subjects will then take more REM sleep than usual when allowed to sleep normally, as if making up for the REM sleep that has been lost. This aspect of making up REM sleep when deprived has important implications for the treatment of nightmares and will be discussed later. Freud, who was working without the benefit of the modern research, thought that the function of dreams was to protect sleep by allowing it to continue uninterrupted. In fact, research results suggest that it may be the other way round. We know that everybody dreams and it may be that REM sleep and the associated dreaming could be an important, even the most important, function of sleeping.

If then, dreaming has an important function, what is it? Research has not produced an answer to the question of why we dream or even why we sleep. Survey results have shown that the common-sense view of sleep is that it is good for us; it helps us to recover from fatigue, is essential for growth and is helpful in curing illness. However, physiological and chemical changes observed during sleep appear to have relatively little to do with actual physical renewal. Certainly our mood and concentration levels worsen rapidly with the loss of one or two nights' sleep, clearly suggesting that sleep does have some function. The idea that we may sleep partly in order to dream has been mentioned above; so what reasons have been suggested to explain dreaming? In the next chapter we will discuss some of the psychological functions and theories of dreaming that have been put forward, but here it is appropriate to mention briefly some of the non-psychological or physiological theories of dream production and function.

One theory, called the 'activation-synthesis hypothesis', proposed by Hobson and McCarley (1977), suggests that physiological processes cause dreams. Specifically these researchers thought that, in REM sleep, the brainstem spontaneously generates random signals, which the cortex attempts to make sense of, in the same way as it makes sense of sensory input while we are awake. It is thought that this interaction gives rise to dreaming and is also responsible for the dream's bizarre characteristics. Critics of this theory have suggested that, although a description of the dreaming process may give an account of the brain's activity, it does not necessarily explain the psychological reason for the process. Hobson has continued, over the years, to propose a physiological basis for dream characteristics. However, Solms (1997) has shown that lesions to parts of the frontal lobe involved in emotional motivation or wishes, or to a sensory area, results in loss of dream recall, but with REM sleep preserved. Thus, he argues, these brain areas seem to be important for creating dreams, with dream production being independent of REM sleep. Another writer who agrees with Hobson is Flanagan (2000), who also considers that dreams are an epiphenomenon.

However, there are several contemporary theories which suggest that dreams have important information and emotion processing functions as well as playing a part in memory consolidation. These theories and arguments have been elegantly summarized by Blagrove (2009) and are only briefly reprised here. Revonuso (2000) envisages dreams as a kind of 'virtual reality' environment in which waking activities, such as threat simulation and avoidance, can be rehearsed. Certainly, many of our dreams are anxiety-producing, suggesting that this may indeed be a function of dreams. Stickgold, Hobson, Fosse and Fosse (2001) describe dreams as 'loose thinking' whereby connections between memories and between emotions and memories, that may not be made in linear waking thinking, are made. This theory makes use of the less focused and more lateral thinking that appears to occur in dreams. Various stages of sleep seem to be involved in memory consolidation but it is not clear whether dreams are involved. However, work by Nielson, Kuiken and Alain (2004) and Nielson and Stenstrom (2005) demonstrated a dream lag effect whereby memories from the previous day, and memories from up to a week ago, reappear in dreams. Nielson suggests that this reappearance of memories in dreams is part of a process of slow consolidation of memories.

In terms of dream content, Freud postulated the 'day residue' incorporation of a previous day's events into dreams. The first person to systematically study the content of dreams was Calvin Hall in the 1950s and 60s. From his extensive content analysis he found that dreamers usually dream about what is going on in their waking lives; this he termed the 'continuity hypothesis'. In fact, bizarreness in dreams occurs relatively infrequently. These findings have been broadly repeated in many studies, particularly by Kramer (2007) and Domhoff (2003). Overall, dreams generally appear to be meaningful, organized and non-random events that reflect the personality and waking life of the dreamer. As yet there is no conclusive evidence for why we dream but it is likely that dreams may serve a variety of physiological and psychological functions. They may be attempts to consolidate memory, process information and resolve emotional preoccupations. Dreams also seem to be metaphorical attempts to deal with current experiences and emotional preoccupations. Even if dreams have no psychological function and/or we don't know for certain why we dream, exploring our dreams can be therapeutically helpful since they reflect waking concerns.

Summary

Since the publication of the first edition there have been considerable developments in the field, including the growth of cognitive therapies and the recent interest of cognitive therapists in working with dreams. Working with trauma and consequently post-traumatic nightmares has also become more important. There is a rich and ancient history of dreamwork that still influences the therapeutic work we do today. Dreaming is largely associated with REM sleep and, while everyone dreams, some have greater recall than others. While some sleep physiologists postulate that dreams are meaningless epiphenomena, contemporary researchers suggest that dreaming may have important information and emotion processing as well as memory consolidation processes. Even if the jury is still out on what the functions of dreaming are, working with dreams can be helpful since they reflect waking concerns.

2

Theories and Models of Dreamwork

Robyn and I began our work on dreams with a lot of information about the historical and current theories of dreams but only one basic assumption, namely, that dreams are the creation of the dreamer. As with any creative product, dreams both reveal aspects of their creator's personality and may be used by their creator to gain insight and foster self-development. We were not committed to any particular theory of dream interpretation but were prepared to foster any approaches or techniques that seemed to fit both the dreamer and the dream, and which could encourage the dreamer ultimately to find her or his own way of integrating dream life and waking life. From the beginning our approach to dreamwork developed thanks to the creative sharing and enthusiasm of many people who attended our workshops, the ideas they sparked off and the opportunities they gave us to link the material they brought with existing information and theory.

Initially the approach adopted was mainly a Gestalt one. This approach will be explained in detail later but it essentially emphasizes 'here and now' methods of bringing dreams to life. Some dreams fitted more readily into this model than others and some people did not find this way of working productive. Gestalt methods are primarily aimed at healing internal splits in the personality, and some of the dream material presented was not about internalized aspects of personality but related to everyday life and the real external world of the dreamer. Faraday's ideas of working with dreams at different levels enriched and amplified the understanding of this material. Her work, outlined in *Dream Power* (1972), emphasized the metaphorical nature of dream symbols. As we developed our interest in the symbolic value of dreams we began to look more closely at the analytic approaches of Freud and Jung. The work of Lillie Weiss and her method of symbolic interpretation, described in *Dream Analysis in Psychotherapy* (1986), was also influential.

Many people described dreams which were long and detailed; the dreams might have many sequences, a long and complicated storyline, or much complex and rich detail. Gestalt methods or approaches that encouraged a purely symbolic interpretation seemed inappropriate here since much material, such as the dream sequences, could be lost. Methods were needed that would bring out the richness of the textual details and so we utilized techniques, which today would be badged as 'cognitive', expounded by Strephon Kaplan Williams in *The Dreamwork Manual* (1984). These methods allowed the dreamer to stand outside the dream and focus on the story, themes, actions, symbols and other relevant aspects, using a wide range of questions aimed at relating the dream contents to the dreamer's life situation.

Another important aspect of the early work in the dream workshops was the sharing of dreams within the group. Often it was the emotional impact of sharing the dream with a supportive group, rather than any specific analysis of the dream state or an interpretation of dream symbols, which was of most value to the dreamer. Hence we looked for effective ways to share dreams in groups. Additionally, we used group imagination to continue the dream story or to elaborate or act out the dream where the dreamer has felt this kind of group input could be helpful.

In the last 20 years the cognitive model has been expanded and developed and as it has done so it has also matured. Early cognitive therapists would probably have seen dreams as the hallmark of psychoanalysis and as such would have eschewed them. Although clients might bring their dreams to cognitive therapy, until the twenty-first century, there was no systematic technique for working with dreams in cognitive therapy. Nevertheless, dreams can be defined as 'the images and thoughts that are experienced during sleep' (Blagrove, 2009: 1), and so it was only a matter of time before creative cognitive therapists were devising, rebadging and adapting dream methods for their purposes. Many of the contemporary methods for working with nightmares, particularly those working with imagery, have been developed within the cognitive model (Hackmann, Bennett-Levy & Holmes, 2011).

The experience of working essentially from an integrationist perspective inevitably leads to looking for the similarities and contrasts between different theories. In following the dream theories over the last 25 years, it is interesting to see how the various models and theories have developed from each other. Much contemporary writing has been based on the work and concepts of Carl Jung, even though much of the groundwork for Jung's theories was laid by Freud. At this stage it is helpful to discuss some of the main theories and models that have been influential in shaping contemporary dreamwork.

Freud's theory of dreams

Freud saw dreams as the 'royal road to the unconscious', where the memories, desires or impulses that were unacceptable to the conscious waking mind were repressed or buried. He understood dreams as largely the product of this unconscious mind and believed that one function of the dream is to preserve sleep by resolving these buried impulses or desires that would otherwise disturb sleep. By examining his own dreams, as well as those of his patients, Freud came to consider that repressed wishes in the unconscious mind found substitute gratification during sleep in the form of dreams. Thus he believed that the dream is a kind of neurotic symptom in its own right. Often, then, the dream reflects the fulfilment of an unsatisfied wish. Freud gave the example of a small boy who dreams of eating a basket of cherries which he was not allowed to eat the day before. In this case the simple, direct wish fulfilment is obvious from the story or 'manifest content' of the dream. However, Freud believed that as people grow older many of the wishes and desires that are associated with earlier stages of development are unable to be fulfilled in reality and so become repressed and generally inaccessible to our conscious mind. He believed that these desires could find fulfilment in the form of a dream but also thought that they would cause us to awaken in intense anxiety, and so he believed that they were disguised. Therefore the dream imagery might symbolize a hidden, or disguised, meaning, which Freud called the 'latent content' of the dream. For example, in an older person the boy eating a basket of cherries might have represented a latent unfulfilled oedipal wish of a boy wishing to possess his mother sexually. The disguise function of dreams not only allows the dreamer to discharge forbidden wishes, but also allows the dreamer to sleep undisturbed by concealing the nature of the wish. Freud saw the dream as functioning both as a guardian of sleep and as a safety valve for unacceptable wishes.

The dreamwork is that process by which the latent content of the dream (its original disguised text) is translated from its manifest content (the text as reported by the dreamer). Freud's method of dream interpretation for arriving at the latent dream thought involved free association, in which the analyst would break the dream down into its different elements and ask the patient to allow his or her mind to roam freely and to say what associations each item has, what recent events it might be connected with and what meaning is suggested. This process might lead a long way from the manifest content of the dream. Freud also based his process of dream interpretation on the belief that certain elements in dreams have a common symbolism for many people. For example, he believed that a house usually represents the human body, kings and queens represent parents, water usually represents birth or life force, and travelling may symbolize dying. Many of Freud's ideas were based on his theory of infantile sexuality, and probably the most well-known, as well as the most misrepresented, of Freud's ideas is that he believed that many symbols had a sexual nature. For example, umbrellas, poles, trees, guns and other similar implements in dreams are thought to represent the penis, while caves, rooms, cupboards and other containers are thought to stand for the vagina and womb.

Faraday (1972) commented that modern research indicated the need to revise Freud's notion of the dual function of dreaming as the guardian of sleep and as a safety valve for repressed wishes. For one thing, there seems little evidence to support the view that all dreams are repressed infantile wishes. In fact, research reports indicate that the majority of our dreams are rather dull and bland. Reporters have noted that many dreams appear to be memories of thoughts and events of the previous day, sometimes called 'day residue', rather than unconscious impulses. Of course it could be argued that this is just a disguise for repressed infantile wishes, but this does not seem a particularly useful viewpoint when a more straightforward interpretation may be more helpful to the dreamer. It is also evident from the literature, as well as from our own dreams and those of our clients, that we often sleep happily through some quite shocking dreams with explicitly sexual or aggressive content which is not particularly disguised. This is not to argue that dreams do not sometimes express wishes either directly or obliquely. However, the fact that we all dream regularly and naturally every night, as well as the fact that we make up REM sleep when we are deprived of it, indicates that rather than dreams being the protector of sleep, one of the functions of sleep may be to allow dreaming.

There has also been controversy over the value of Freud's work for women. As early as 1981, Ernst and Goodison commented that the male bias of traditional Freudian thinking may lead to women's dreams being misinterpreted in a distorted way, especially since it is evident that the analyst's own views and prejudices inevitably will affect the interpretation made. Ernst and Goodison also questioned whether patients, of either gender, get the chance to fully 'feel' the emotional content of the dream and how much use they can make of the interpretation given to them. They believed that the meaning of the dream cannot be reduced to a disguised thought, capable of being spelled out in words. As Jung and later theorists believed, a dream can speak to us in a different language, revealing conflicts, feelings or buried parts of our personalities.

Many authors have also criticized Freud's view of the sexual nature of symbols. Few dreamworkers now believe that certain symbols regularly stand for certain elements and most object to the reduction of all symbols to a single idea. Especially as it has been popularized, this approach often degenerates into interpreting dreams mechanically from an index of symbols and fails to allow for individual or cultural change. Symbols are determined in part by the society and situation we live in, but can vary from one individual to another and within each of us over time, changing as we change.

Although there are some shortcomings in Freud's original theory and method of dream interpretation, it should be remembered that Freud himself was analysing dreams of patients coming to him for treatment and that most dream interpretation should be seen within the context of an ongoing analysis. Also Freud was working without the benefit of modern dream research. All the dream writers agree that Freud's theory of dreams was a crucial landmark and laid the groundwork on which most subsequent theories are based. Jung's theory, described next, is a development and extension of Freud's theory.

Jung's theory of dreams

A crucial difference between Jung and Freud, and one which accounts for much of the popularity of Jung's views, is his belief that the dream is a normal, creative expression of the unconscious, rather than Freud's perception of the dream as a disturbed mental activity. Jung thought that dreams frequently reflected the workings of an inner drive towards health and maturity and believed this was a drive with which the conscious mind could cooperate. He also emphasized that symbols cannot be reduced to set formulas, but encouraged exploring the quality and texture of a symbol rather than the meaning behind it. Thus, rather than seeing a symbol as a disguise for something else, Jung believed symbols should be recognized as having power in their own right and therefore laid more emphasis on the manifest content of dreams to see what they revealed rather than what they were hiding. Jung believed that pictures and symbols are the natural language of the unconscious and that a dream symbol expresses a psychic fact which can only partially be described in verbal and rational terms. So he laid less emphasis on the interpretation of a dream, and felt that the experiencing of the telling of a dream was an important therapeutic process in itself. Jung looked to religious myths and legends in his search for the most significant symbols of the human mind; he believed that universal themes revealed the existence in each individual of a layer of the mind common to the whole universe. He called this 'the collective unconscious'. Archetypes of the collective unconscious are expressions of the fundamental and perennial interests of humankind which are so pervasive as to appear in the symbolism and languages of many people. Examples of archetypal symbols will be given in the next chapter.

Because Jung did not think that all dreams were infantile sexual wish-fulfilment needs, he emphasized the present situation in the life of the dreamer. He thought that dreams are a self-representation of the unconscious mind of the dreamer and that each element or symbol portrays a mood, emotion or part of the dreamer's personality. He believed that the 'I' in the dream represents the conscious ego of the dreamer. For Jung the function of the dream was to restore our psychological equilibrium. Ernst and Goodison (1981: 6) quote the example of a patient with a high opinion of himself who dreamed he was a tramp lying in a ditch. According to Jung this dream was attempting to balance the one-sided picture the man usually presented to the world. He called this the 'compensatory role' of dreams. Jung disagreed with Freud's method of free association, which he felt could lead away from the story of the dream. He did not have one clear method of dream interpretation but felt that the dream was interpreted when it made sense to the dreamer. He often worked with a series of dreams rather than a single dream and used a variety of meditative, artistic and imaginative methods which he felt would amplify the story and meaning of the dream.

Although Jung's ideas form the clearest basis for many contemporary methods, they do have some limitations. Whereas Freud probably overestimated the role played by repressed sexuality in dreams, Jung probably underestimated the sexual element. There is little reference in his work to the body and physical sensations. Also, it is possible that the classical and literary references in Jung's writings may seem to imply that those of us without the benefit of a classical or literary education may not be able to interpret our own dreams. Indeed, some people have been put off by his somewhat esoteric style of writing. Nevertheless, Jung's theories do bring dream interpretation within the range of any of us: we do not have to be analysts to understand our own dreams. Most of all, Jung's theories of dreams show a respect for the unconscious. Rather than a repository of shameful events and thoughts, Jung represents dreams as an abundantly creative treasure trove with the potential to strengthen the personality. For those readers wishing to pursue Jung's theories in greater depth, helpful books are Jung's *Man and His Symbols* (1978) and *Dreams* (2002).

Perls's Gestalt theory of dreams

Fritz Perls, who founded the Gestalt school of therapy and who died in 1970, developed and extended Jung's theory of dreams. Although he was originally trained as a Freudian, Perls rejected the idea of the unconscious and focused on the 'here and now' present verbal and non-verbal behaviour of the dreamer. Whereas Freud described the dream as the 'royal road to the unconscious', Perls called dreams the 'royal road to integration' because he believed that by working with dreams we can reclaim the lost parts of our personality and become more integrated or whole. Perls viewed the dream as an existential message, as opposed to Freud's view of the dream as wishful thinking. He saw the main function of dreams as being to resolve unfinished situations and to integrate fragments of our personalities. He believed that each character or object in a dream is a part of us, a fragment of our personality that we have projected out of ourselves. He believed that people needed to re-own each of these fragmented parts of the personality in order to become a whole.

The Gestalt method is to bring a dream to life by having the dreamer tell the dream in the first person, present tense as if it were happening now and then to identify with, and speak as, each element in the dream. The different characters or parts of the dream may then dialogue with each other. The technique usually involves each dream item occupying a different chair, and the dreamer moving between chairs as she or he conducts the dialogue, in an attempt to identify and ultimately integrate the conflicting parts of the personality. Perls introduced the concepts of 'topdog' and 'underdog'; the topdog is the parental, critical and self-righteous part of the personality that makes unrealistic demands of the underdog, which is the whining, child-like, manipulative part of the personality. Often the two parts are locked into a struggle and a dream dialogue turns into a topdog/underdog conflict. Perls felt that by acting out this conflict people may be able to integrate the two aspects of themselves. Perls's theory is similar to Jung's theory in so far as the characters and items in a dream are viewed as repressed parts of the dreamer's personality. Using Perls's method, the dreamer acts out these repressed parts in order to re-own aspects of the personality which have been alienated, and thus to come to a fuller and stronger sense of the self as a whole personality. So Gestalt therapy is a vivid method for bringing disconnected or discredited parts of ourselves into awareness. Perls believed that each time we identify with some part of a dream, turning 'it' into 'I', vital energy is reclaimed.

While Gestalt methodology can be immensely productive, even with snippets or fragments of dream material, it has some limitations. For instance, it can take the dreamer a long way from the narrative of the dream, and it is unlikely that even the most energetic or enthusiastic person can act out and dialogue with each element in a long and complex dream. Despite these limitations, the method can be very helpful for working with nightmares or recurring dreams, since they are likely to reflect long-standing conflicts or splits within the personality, triggered off by some present life situation of the dreamer. The techniques can be used individually, although they are often very powerful in a group setting. Gestalt methodology can be extremely powerful and when a dreamer works in the first person and the present tense he or she can be encouraged to connect quickly and directly to their feelings.

Faraday's theory of dreams

Ann Faraday, whose first book *Dream Power* was published in 1972, utilized many Jungian and Gestalt concepts. She emphasized that dreams can reflect the present life situation of the dreamer and also largely rejected the wish-fulfilment and disguise elements of Freudian theory. Her main contribution from our point of view was her belief that a dream could be interpreted at different levels, and this can be a helpful approach for the therapist to adopt. Faraday identified three levels ('looking outward', 'through the looking glass' and 'looking inward') and believed that a comprehensive approach to dream interpretation could be achieved by examining a dream from any one of the three standpoints to be described and selecting the method of interpretation most suitable. Like Perls, she also felt that a dream was interpreted when it felt satisfactory to the dreamer.

Faraday called her first level 'looking outward' and believed that, at this level, dreams may provide objective truth about the outside world. She thought that the sensible procedure was, initially, to look at any dream to see if it could be throwing up real information about external events which have not been assimilated by the conscious mind in waking life. Such dreams are usually triggered by subliminal perceptions picked up during the day but not consciously registered by the waking mind. Faraday stated that dreams that give the most useful message at this level are usually warnings and reminders, and her book contains many examples. The following is an example from one of our dreams:

> Robyn, returning from a driving holiday abroad, found it necessary to switch on the rear demister; she thought to herself that she must not forget to switch it off. Some time later she pulled into a motorway service station for a short sleep and dreamed that she was driving along when she was passed by a car full of people all gesticulating and pointing at her rear window. She awoke and realized that she had left her rear demister on. For her this was the essential message of the dream.

Faraday called her second level 'through the looking glass'. This is a reference to *Alice Through the Looking Glass* by Lewis Carroll, and means that the dream can act as a distorting mirror which has twisted external reality according to the dreamer's inner attitudes and conflicts, and can give a picture of the dreamer's own unique reality. Thus, through the looking glass of our dreams we receive messages about our subjective reactions to the people and situations in the external world. Faraday comments that all dreams are, in a way, pictures of subjective reality, but some have more objective validity than others and it is up to the dreamer to decide where the energy is.

> Nazir had a dream in which he was having a blazing row with his father. On the surface this appeared uncharacteristic of the relationship in waking life, which generally was controlled and restrained. On reflection, Nazir began to realize that the dream was revealing some of the things that he would actually like to say to his father, but which he refrained from saying in waking life for many reasons.

The third level of dream interpretation, according to Faraday, is the level at which dreams can give insight into the dreamer's deepest self. She called this level 'looking inward' and believed that such dreams concern conflicts which are not primarily with characters in the external world but rather with internal conflicts or split-off portions of the self. For working at this level Faraday suggests using Gestalt techniques.

> Maggie reported a dream in which the Queen was visiting her house for tea. Despite all Maggie's efforts to tidy up, piles of little pieces of paper kept appearing in places where she had just tidied. Maggie set up an imaginary dialogue between herself and the Queen. During the dialogue it became apparent that the Queen

represented the authoritarian parts of Maggie's own mother which she had intro-jected, or taken into herself, in her desire to be neat and tidy. When Maggie dia-logued with the untidy piles of paper, she realized that these represented the creative parts of herself which were not willing to be tidied away. Maggie later revealed that, although she had been good at writing, she had been discouraged from pursuing it as a career.

It is, of course, possible to analyze the same dream at different levels, and while there are no absolute guidelines that will determine at which level it is appropriate to work, there are some hints which will be explored later.

Cognitive theories of dreams

Cognitive therapy, first expounded by Aaron T. Beck in the 1960s, attempts to help the client by identifying and changing dysfunctional thinking, behaviour and feelings. (Beck, Rush, Shaw and Emery, 1979). Therapy is based on collaboration between therapist and client and on empirically testing beliefs. This may be done by testing the client's, often unquestioned, assumptions and by identifying those that are distorted, unrealistic and unhelpful. Once these, for the most part automatic, thoughts have been challenged then the feelings around these thoughts are more easily changed. Beck's early work centred on depression, and he believed that depressed people acquire a negative schema of the world in childhood and adolescence. A schema can be described as a structured cluster of pre-conceived ideas. A depressed person might acquire a nega-tive schema through a number of difficult early events such as the loss of a parent, criticism by parents or teachers, bullying, rejection and other negative events. When a person with such schemas meets a situation that, in some way, resembles the original situation, the negative schemas of the person are activated. Beck's negative triad posits that depressed people have negative experiences about themselves, their experiences in the world, and the future. Beck also described what he termed 'cognitive distortions' or errors in thinking which can all contribute to depression. Examples of these are all-or-nothing thinking, over-generalization, and selective perception.

Beck was also theorizing about dreams as early as the 1960s (Beck & Ward, 1961) and formulated a cognitive behavioural therapy (CBT) method in 1971 (Beck, 1971). He initially regarded dreams in the clinical context as a kind of snapshot or 'biopsy' of a client's dysfunctional sche-mata that were analogous to automatic thoughts. He also suggested that focusing on the more obvious or 'manifest' content of dreams was more satisfactory than trying to infer hidden meanings. He understood a client's dreams as 'idiosyncratic and dramatic expressions of the patient's view of self, the world, and the future (what Beck termed the "cognitive triad")'

(Freeman & White, 2004: 74). Since dream material reflected the cognitive triad, it followed that the dream would also demonstrate the client's cognitive distortions. Doweiko (1982) used rational emotive therapy (RET) to encourage the client to directly challenge depressive cognitions reflected in the dream. Following the cognitive tradition, dreams can be thought of as core cognitive schemas (J. S. Beck, 1995) or early maladaptive schemas (Young, 1999).

Contemporary cognitive writers have been debating a distinction between objectivist and constructivist views of cognitive therapy (e.g. Neimeyer & Stewart, 2000). Constructivist philosophy emphasizes both personal and social processes of meaning. In particular the individual is seen as an active participant in construing reality rather than on reflecting or representing reality. This rather vague definition of constructivism has meant that it might be seen as a meta-theory that has influenced a number of psychotherapies including existential-humanistic therapies, personal construct psychotherapy (PCP), and narrative therapy as well as CBT.

Recent cognitive writers on dreams (Rosner et al., 2004) suggest that cognitive dream methodology can be divided into basic epistemologies: objectivist and constructivist. Adherents of the 'objectivist' tradition believe that the rational and logical manipulations of classical cognitive therapy should be used to challenge those assumptions and beliefs associated with a client's dream. For example, Doweiko (2004) and Freeman and White (2004) argue that dreams are amenable to the same cognitive restructuring and reality testing procedures that can be applied to a client's waking automatic thoughts and belief. Adherents of what Rosner et al. (2004) describe as 'constructivist' approaches encourage clients to enter into the metaphorical, subjective and affective experiences in their dreams, consistent with the constructionist perspective. For example, Barrett (2004) argues that dreams function as powerful, condensed metaphors, and that modern, psychodynamic dreamwork can act as a useful shortcut for getting at a client's idiosyncratic cognitive patterns and meanings. Another example of a constructivist approach, included by Rosner et al. in their book (2004), is Hill's (1996, 2004) cognitive-experiential method of dream interpretation. This model is an integrative model that has evolved from a number of different theoretical orientations. It involves three stages: exploration, insight and action.

From the above it can be seen that there is no one cognitive method but rather a broad collection of methods used by cognitive therapists, 'particularly therapists working at the intersection of cognitive therapy and other therapeutic traditions' (Rosner et al., 2004: 3). Dowd writes that 'cognitive therapy in the early 21st century is a great deal more than talk. It involves nonverbal cognitions (imagery) as well as embodiment techniques' (2004: xi). It is also clear that cognitive theorists have an increasingly integrationist perspective which fits well with the integrative approach of this book. Coincidentally, the first edition of this book also divided dream methodologies into two broad categories, 'objective' and 'subjective' approaches, very similar to those described above. Therefore it makes conceptual sense to integrate cognitive methods into the current structure of the book and examples of some of the cognitive methods mentioned above will be described in detail, with examples, in the chapters that follow.

An integrationist model of dreamwork

The background to the integrative model and the theories most influential in shaping it have been described, and it will be clear that it is based on a number of sources. It is also highly congruent with the principles underlying cognitive approaches but is not bound by any one tradition and is thus truly integrative. The principles are:

1   A dream is the personal creation of the dreamer and, as such, belongs to the dreamer and is available for them to use in any way they choose.
2   The dreamer is free to tell their dream story in a way that makes sense to them. Therefore it is unhelpful for a therapist to rigidly impose an approach or technique and it is suggested that together therapist and client select an appropriate method from a range of approaches.
3   The dream is satisfactorily 'interpreted' when it makes sense to the dreamer.
4   A dream does not have to be interpreted by 'professionals' and the dreamer can use most of the methods that we will describe by themselves. It is also true that a co-worker or therapist skilled and experienced in dreamwork methods may provide more effective help from the dreamer's point of view.
5   Dreams may represent early material that develops in childhood and that exists at the periphery of consciousness not directly or immediately accessible to the dreamer.
6   Dreams reflect the concerns, worries and desires of our conscious, waking lives.
7   Dreams are messages from a part of our conscious selves that speak verbally, visually and metaphorically.
8   Dreams can offer direct access to cognitive and affective processes – the clients' cognitive and affective schemata; they could be termed 'dream thoughts' or 'dream feelings'. Cognitive, analytic or experiential approaches can be used.
9   Dreams are not regarded as neurotic symptoms indicating pathology. Therefore the approach adopted is a psychological humanistic model indicating that dreams can be used therapeutically or creatively in a striving towards wholeness.
10 As well as using methods accessible and acceptable to the dreamer, it is important to use methods appropriate to the nature of the dream itself.
11 Dreams can be interpreted at any level. The level of interpretation is usually indicated by the nature of the dream material and/or the wishes and feelings of the dreamer. The skills of the therapist are also relevant here.
12 It is often therapeutically helpful, though not essential, for the dream to be 'actualized' in waking life. That means that the dreamer formulates an action or a decision from the dream that can be carried into waking life.

Summary

The background to the integrationist approach adopted by Robyn Sewell and myself and the theories shaping it have been described. This is followed by an explanation of the two classic theories of Freud and Jung, as well as their strengths and limitations. Two theories, particularly helpful for exploring dreams, and developing out of Freud and Jung's ideas, namely those of Fritz Perls and Ann Faraday, are described. This is then followed by an outline of the main ideas of the cognitive model of dreams and a brief outline of its broad collection of methods. Finally, the principles of an integrationist model of dreamwork, which underpin the dreamwork in this book, have been outlined.

3

The Language of Dreams

Before proceeding to a detailed discussion of dreamwork techniques it is helpful for the reader to have an understanding of the more traditional methods of symbolic interpretation that apply to some of these techniques. The later chapters of methods are divided into what have been called 'objective' and 'subjective and constructivist' approaches; one chapter will be devoted to each of these approaches. Essentially, objective methods require the dreamer to stand outside the dream and explore the cognitions, feelings and themes, whereas subjective methods require the dreamer to attempt to 'get inside' the dream in an experiential way and 'bring it to life'. In this chapter some of the general principles of dream language that underpin the objective approaches are discussed.

Principles of symbolic interpretation

Psychoanalytic approaches to symbolic interpretation

There are many ways to interpret dream symbols and different workers have placed different emphases on the more universal nature of certain symbols compared to their private meaning. Freud used free association as his main method for dream interpretation and, whilst this enables the client to explore their private meanings, it also tends to take them away from the actual dream material. It is also true that Freud had his own theories about the meanings of many dream symbols, and since he related dreams primarily to the expression of unconscious wish-fulfilment of suppressed 'Id', or instinctual, fantasies, these were often sexual in nature. It is often the case that Freudian analysts will work towards helping their clients to accept the universal nature and meanings of their dream symbols.

Whilst Jung highlighted the revealing, as opposed to the concealing, aspect of symbols and emphasized the more personal and changing nature of symbols, he too linked dreams into his broader philosophy. He thus posited certain universal aspects of interpretation (e.g. archetypes). As a result of the work of both Freud and Jung, as well as other psychoanalysts, there have appeared a number of dream dictionaries such as Tom Chetwynd's *Dictionary for Dreamers* (1974). While such dictionaries can occasionally be helpful, most contemporary dreamworkers do not believe that dream symbols can be interpreted mechanically from a dictionary. Dreamers have to explore the personal meanings of their own symbols. The cognitive view of dreams is that the content is idiosyncratic to the dreamer, and certainly the idea of universal symbols would not be accepted within this model and is not the view adopted in this book.

The process of interpretation is an attempt to bring unconscious material into conscious awareness. In dream terms this means taking the actual dream story (the manifest dream content) and looking for the underlying (latent or unconscious) meaning. It is not necessary to hold any particular theoretical position concerning the nature of the unconscious but simply to differentiate between those cognitions that are directly or easily accessible to awareness, and those which are less directly accessible. These cognitions may be less directly accessible by virtue of remoteness in time, because they are infrequently used and so less familiar, or maybe because they have entered the memory bank without due (conscious) processing. The notion of repression of traumatic or unacceptable memories as well as other manifestations of defence mechanisms can also be accepted. An assumption is made that dreams do not respond to such boundaries and therefore are a potent means of revealing aspects of ourselves that, for one reason or another, may not be directly accessible in our waking lives.

A dreamworker whose approach was drawn upon heavily in developing the methods developed by Robyn Sewell and myself is Lillie Weiss. In her book *Dream Analysis in Psychotherapy* (1986), Weiss outlines a method for dream interpretation which involves a literal translation from the manifest (story) content of the dream into the latent (underlying meaning) content. The main feature of this method is that literally every dream symbol (i.e. every object, action or quality) is interpreted. The dream is then reconstructed in terms of these new (latent) meanings. Emotions do not fall clearly into the category of symbols as they tend to form a link between the manifest and latent content and, in themselves, can act as important clues in the process of translation. Often, as the story unfolds, unsolved symbols and meanings begin to make sense, and the feelings associated with each aspect or scene in the dream can add clarity to the meaning. However, it is important to warn the would-be dream interpreter that straightforward translations of this nature do not invariably occur and it may be necessary to work on subsequent dreams for the dream meaning and message to emerge clearly. Later in the chapter some of the rules, or grammar, of dream language that can facilitate the process of symbol translation will be discussed.

Cognitive approaches to symbolic interpretation

The view of many cognitive workers is that the dream can speak to us directly without the use of symbols (Rosner et al., 2004). Beck (1971) believed that working on the manifest content is more helpful than trying to infer underlying processes that may be vague or inaccessible. Beck also thought that, since the dream content is readily available to the dreamer, working on this can allow a client a sense of mastery rather than depending on an 'expert' to interpret the symbolism of the dream (Freeman & White, 2004). As was described earlier, Beck considered that dream content and language reflected the cognitive triad and thus the client's cognitive distortions and schemata. Freeman and White also comment that Beck followed Alfred Adler, who also believed that dream themes 'are directly relevant to the patient's waking life and identified behavioural experience. Dreams are a product of the dreamer's internal world, but they maintain an essential continuity with the waking thought process' (2004: 74). Therefore, Freeman and White offer guidelines for dreamwork in CBT, some of which are:

1   The dream needs to be understood in thematic rather than symbolic terms.
2   The thematic content of the dream is idiosyncratic to the dreamer and must be viewed within the context of the dreamer's life.
3   The specific language and imagery of the dream are important to the meaning.
4   The affective responses to the dreams can be seen as similar to the dreamer's affective responses in waking situations.
5   The dream material and images will reflect the client's schema.
6   Dream content, language and images are amenable to the same cognitive restructuring as automatic thoughts. (Adapted from Freeman & White, 2004: 85)

> Eva had a dream in which she was driving down a road with her partner beside her. She suddenly found that she was paralysed and the car was skidding and going out of control. She was very distressed and called out 'help me, help me' but her partner, Patrick, didn't respond or make a move to help her. She woke up in a panic. In discussion in the therapy session Eva talked about her feelings of not being in control as well as her wish that her partner would be more proactive in taking control of more in their relationship by being more 'in the driving seat'. In life Eva was somewhat passive, often waiting for things to happen; she also had a belief that she shouldn't ask for what she needed. In therapy she worked on being more assertive with her partner as well as on taking more control proactively in her own life. She was able to rescript her dream in two ways. In the first version Eva was on her own in the car and was able to keep it under control in difficult and icy conditions; in the second version of the re-dream Eva asked Patrick to help when the car skidded and he leaned over and took the wheel and successfully brought the car under control again.

Humanistic approaches to symbolic interpretation

Another theory that does not subscribe to the notion that each dream symbol needs to be 'translated' in order to find the latent content or meaning is that of Ann Faraday. In the previous chapter, Ann Faraday's theory of three levels of interpretation, which she named respectively 'looking outwards', 'through the looking glass' and 'looking inwards', were described. The first two levels are capable of speaking directly to the dreamer and may require little or no translation, since the dream itself is the message.

Level one, 'looking outwards', deals with day residue. Dreams of this type usually occur during the early cycles of sleep and relate in a relatively direct manner to events of the preceding day. These dreams seem to be related to the initial stages of processing short-term memories and often contain material which is directly recognizable as belonging to recent waking events. These might be people or activities that the dreamer has been involved with during the day, possibly an image from a television programme, a conversation or an everyday activity such as mowing the lawn or ironing. As was noted in the previous chapter, Faraday suggests that the dream material of this stage contains an objective truth concerning perceptions, thoughts or ideas that the dreamer had not properly consciously processed during the day. These may be thinly disguised; for example, a dream of a house blowing up may be connected with an awareness of an electric plug which is in a dangerous state but has not been repaired. Faraday suggests that when we do recall such dreams we check with the objective reality. While recognizing that even the most mundane scenarios might symbolically represent deep and important truths, the suggestion is that it is not worth investing much energy in interpreting this kind of dream. The reality is that dreamers tend to forget this type of material rather quickly and rarely feel intrigued enough to present it for interpretation.

The second level, 'through the looking glass', does present more food for thought, but very often the literal meaning of the dream contains the message and few symbolic interpretations are necessary. These dreams are often about people, relationships and feelings, and these can be read for what they are; the symbols are fairly obvious. Faraday suggests that if the person or subject in the dream concerns a person or event in one's current life, the dream can best be understood in terms of the hitherto unacknowledged aspects of those relationships or events. The next dream is a good illustration of this.

> Bob's dream occurred while he was at a business convention with a large number of colleagues, some of whom he had known for many years. One of these colleagues, Alf, was an acquaintance whom Bob had met on a number of occasions in a formal or semi-formal setting. Alf had always seemed to Bob to be affable, friendly, socially at ease and a person with whom it was pleasant to be in company. In the dream Alf was blindfolded and standing against a wall, about to be shot by a firing squad. Bob, as the dream ego (the person from whose point of view the

dream is told), was standing nearby. As the time for the execution approached, Alf beckoned Bob to his side and began whispering to him: 'Now that I have nothing more to lose I want you to know what I am really like.' Alf then gave Bob an account of his life of duplicity, business double-dealings, and generally cynical attitudes that were at complete variance with his non-dream appearance. When Bob thought about this dream on waking, he realized immediately that it reflected a hitherto unformulated suspicion that Alf was not all he appeared to be; in fact, he had seemed 'too good to be true'. Bob had occasionally wondered about the honesty of some of Alf's business dealings. The effect of this dream had no wider repercussions than to bring this attitude to the forefront of Bob's mind and to cause him to treat Alf in a more circumspect manner on future occasions when they met.

This dream about Alf could also have been interpreted through translation of specific symbols. Alternatively, it could have been subjected to a Gestalt approach which would perhaps have revealed more about the dreamer himself than an actual relationship existing in his waking life. This would have taken us to Faraday's third level of interpretation, which, as described in the last chapter, is called 'looking inward' and posits that dreams concern conflicts within the self. A Gestalt approach, more suitable for this level of interpretation, will be described in detail in a later chapter. The point here is that a meaning which satisfied the dreamer presented itself rapidly and in a way that brought a semiconscious awareness into fully conscious awareness. Bob did not feel it necessary to probe any further at this time.

Bob's choice of level of interpretation highlights the point that many dreams can be interpreted at different levels. Along with most other contemporary dream approaches, an integrationist model holds very strongly that a dream is correctly interpreted when it makes sense to the dreamer, whether or not other aspects or levels of interpretation seem more obvious to the therapist. This underlies a very basic assumption that the dream 'belongs' to the dreamer and is correctly interpreted when it makes sense to her or him. This is not to say that dreamers may not choose to go back to the original dream and rework the material, perhaps exploring the therapist's suggestions, but the choice is up to them. The purpose of the dreamwork outlined in this book is to help individuals to become more aware of aspects of themselves, their thoughts, feelings or events in their lives, which have hitherto been unacknowledged or only half-recognized. Dream interpretation should ideally lead to a decision to act in real life; that is, the dream should be actualized. This cannot be done if the dreamer does not take full responsibility for (or 'own') the interpretation.

From a practical point of view, it is never possible to make manifest every conceivable level of interpretation present in a dream. Jeremy Taylor in his book *Dream Work* (1983) suggests that there are 25 basic elements contained in every dream. These may include: elements of libidinous sexual desire, unconscious wish-fulfilment, reflections of physical health and state of the body, day residue, childhood reminiscences, speculations about the future, archetypal drama, creative inspiration or problem solving. Clearly it is not helpful to look for all these elements in every dream.

In one example, Suzanne, a middle-aged woman, reported two dreams involving streams of blood flowing. In the first dream she had lost a tooth and started bleeding profusely from her mouth, although she felt no pain. The blood flowed in a stream, down her body, into a large tub. The second dream, three nights later, was specifically about menstruation. In the dream she was in a public place and again a stream of blood was flowing from her, which she found, much to her surprise, was coming from her vagina. In working on these dreams she revealed that they had occurred at a time when she had just started hormone replacement therapy (HRT). She said that she had been surprised when the doctor had warned her that she would start having periods again, but had not given it much thought at the time. However, the changes occurring in her body as a result of the treatment began to insinuate themselves into her awareness via the medium of the dreams described. The resulting action of this dreamwork was simply to stimulate Suzanne to think through the full implications of her treatment. There are many other symbolic meanings that could be taken from these dreams, but in this instance the reflection of the body state made sense to Suzanne and other explanations were not sought.

Dream language

In our dreamwork using objective approaches Robyn Sewell and I came to recognize that dreams display a grammatical structure similar to language. The structure is more illogical and inconsistent than that of other languages; nevertheless, there are a certain number of grammatical 'rules' which can help us in our interpretation. The following guidelines are based on the work of Lillie Weiss (1986) and Ann Faraday (1974).

Dream symbols

Every dream image and action can be read as a symbol for something else. The act of interpretation involves finding the common characteristic that is shared by both manifest and latent meaning. For example, Robyn often dreams of dogs. In real life dogs represent for her 'unconditional friendliness'. Very often, but not invariably, this aspect of being a 'dream friend' is what they represent in her dreams. This association of friendliness and dogs may be relevant for many people, and so has a common or shared symbolic meaning. To some extent, however, it also has a personal meaning, since for many people dogs may represent other things. For example, they can represent something frightening or menacing, dependency, mess, stupidity, faithfulness and so on. Indeed, in Jung's archetypes, animals in dreams frequently represent the 'animal' part of ourselves, the untamed, primitive, instinctual aspects of our nature that are usually suppressed as we try to live by the rules of civilized society. So when we look for symbolic meanings in our dreams, it is important to remember that symbols have personal meanings for every individual. However, to the extent that we share a common culture, or even a common human heritage, the symbols may have a common meaning. A search for the common meaning can be very helpful when the dreamer is completely stuck. For example, a dove is commonly known as a symbol for peace. Therefore, a reminder to the dreamer who has dreamed of a dove that the dove is a harbinger of peace may be helpful. The important point to remember is that the common meaning should never be imposed on the personal meaning. A dove could, after all, have a personal sinister meaning for a particular individual.

It is not only objects that act as symbols in dreams. People may equally well represent somebody or something else. Faraday suggests that, if the person is not somebody who is actually involved in the dreamer's current life, then it is advisable to look for the symbolic value of that person in the dream. For example, people often dream of a dead grandparent, and sometimes the symbolic meaning turns out to be somebody who is very wise, or loving, or reassuring because those are the qualities that grandparents have represented to the dreamer when she or he was a child.

Many other elements in dreams have symbolic importance and should not be ignored. These include actions, vivid colours, numbers, names and spoken words.

John dreamed he was on a bus journey on a 'greyish-green' bus. He was not sure where or why he was travelling. In this case the 'greyish-green' colour of the bus provided an important clue, since John recalled that he often went to visit his father on a 'Grey-Green Line' London bus. This immediately established the context of the dream for John, and interpretation of the rest of the dream became easy.

Jo, on the other hand, recounted a dream which took place in the college where she was currently a mature student. The dream was about a conversation she was having with a fellow student, and it took place in Room 265 at the college. Jo was mystified, since the conversation did not make sense in her current life, and the college had no room number 265. This dream was recounted to a group, a member of which was particularly interested in the significance of numbers. At her instigation the group members addressed themselves to the symbolic meaning of 265. Many abortive suggestions were made, until somebody suggested that we think about dates. Jo's reaction was immediate: 'My parents are coming to visit me on the 26th May. This makes sense now! The conversation is with my mother, not with another student, and I know this is right because, now I come to think of it, there is a little table in the room which has nothing to do with college, but which belongs in my parents' home.' Further work on this dream led Jo to explore the idea that her mother disapproved of Jo 'neglecting' her children in order to pursue her own studies. Ultimately Jo was able to confront some of her underlying feelings of guilt about this matter.

Dream symbols are often vivid, humorous or frightening. They are capable of putting into concrete imagery quite complex ideas, thoughts or feelings.

Dramatization

One of the common aspects of dream language is the use of drama. This is an exaggeration of reality, whereby dream elements can be portrayed as larger than life. This can be rather frightening to people who are unused to dream language. For example, a disagreement between partners can be displayed in the dream as an actual battle.

> Helena was dismayed to find herself, in a dream, as part of an army inside a fortress lobbing grenades over the walls onto her partner in the opposing side. She was relieved to discover that this might be the dream's way of bringing into awareness the importance to Helena of an ongoing dispute with her partner over moving to a different area.

Education about aspects of dream language can be helpful and reassuring to clients who are beginning to explore their dreams but are frightened or embarrassed by their dream contents. Often the use of dramatization in dreams can exaggerate dream elements to absurd degrees. This element of the ridiculous can often be humorous and help to put the issue into perspective for the client.

> Lynn dreamed that, on entering her local church, she was surprised to discover that her partner had been made a saint. There was an enormous plaster statue of him, so large that it was entirely out of proportion. When working with this dream Lynn was amused by the exaggeration of the importance she put on her partner's good qualities. Of course a 'plaster saint' is an interesting symbol in its own right. The point about dramatization is that the statue was exaggerated out of all proportion.

Condensation and dilation

In a dream several different ideas and impressions may be condensed into a single compact image.

> Trudi's dream was of her house. Although many features of the house confirmed her impression that this was the modern house in England where she lived with her husband and children, the dream house contained a heavy carved oak door which belonged to her childhood home in another country. In working on the dream the door came to represent a psychological barrier which emanated from her childhood and was now affecting her relationship with her present family.

Dilation is the reverse of condensation and occurs when the same image or message is repeated, in perhaps a different symbolic form, over and over in the same dream. This often appears in the form of a frustrated activity or journey as in Brendan's dream.

> Brendan found himself setting out on a train journey across a desert. The train broke down and he continued his journey in a jeep. However, the jeep ran out of petrol and he continued his journey on horseback. Finally, when the horse fell, Brendan found himself struggling to walk through sinking sand. Although at first Brendan could not make sense of the dream, in therapy he was able to look at the repeated theme of a frustrated journey. This led him to explore his feelings of being 'stuck' and ideas that he was powerless to affect this since people kept letting him down.

> In another example, Jean recounted a dream of moving to a new house and finding her young nieces responsible for an act of irritation or vandalism in every room she entered, such that it frustrated her enjoyment of her new home. Once she had identified the common theme, Jean was able to work on an area of frustration with her sister, who, in the dream, had been responsible for bringing the messy children into Jean's nice new home.

Common themes and symbols

The danger of assuming that symbols have a meaning common to everybody has already been stressed. However, if we are judicious in our use of commonly accepted interpretations, we can find them helpful, especially when we work out our own personal meanings. Freud's symbols were often sexual in nature, but not invariably so. His idea that a dream house can represent the dreamer's body can often lead to very fruitful interpretations, as can the identification of flowing water with giving birth, literally or metaphorically. Because many English people used to regard members of the Royal Family as ultimate authority figures, dreaming of one of them could often be symbolic of our own early, all-powerful authority figures, whether it be mother, father or other parent figure. An example of this was Maggie's dream in the previous chapter. The most powerful of common themes and symbols are to be found in Jung's archetypes. Occasionally somebody will present a powerful symbolic dream that appears to be what Jung termed a 'big dream' in which archetypal material seems to dominate. A detailed exploration of Jungian symbols and archetypes requires a level of specialized study and knowledge that goes beyond the scope and needs of most contemporary therapists working from an integrationist perspective. Nevertheless, some concepts can be valuable to us in our work because of the frequency with which they are reported. These are the 'persona', or mask we wear to present ourselves to the world, the 'shadow', or part of us that is denied and repressed, and the 'animus/anima', the deep identification with the opposite sex that each of us carries within ourselves. Those who are interested can pursue a deeper understanding of Jungian symbols, whilst noting that Jung himself emphasized the personal and changing nature of dream symbols (Jung, 2002).

Metaphors

The symbolic meaning of a dream can often be found by looking for the metaphoric meaning of a dream image or action. A metaphor is defined as a figure of speech in which a term is transferred to something to which it does not literally apply. Dream images often give a literal meaning to a thought or action which, once translated back into colloquial speech, can give us an understanding of what the dream is about.

> Kerri had a dream in which she was skating on a pond in her garden. She was aware as she moved that she could see water ahead and wondered if she was safe enough to reach the gate which she could see ahead of her at the end of the garden. The literal meaning of the dream (the image of her 'skating on thin ice') was explored for its metaphorical meaning. Kerri associated this with a number of short-cuts that she was taking in her work and recognized an underlying, but hitherto unexpressed, worry that something might go badly wrong. Having made this initial association, Kerri was able to work out a number of other symbols contained in the scene and to understand the meaning and message of the dream.

We use many other metaphorical phrases unthinkingly in our everyday speech, and many of these have been reported as themes very frequently in workshops and by clients. It is often useful to look for these at an early stage in the interpretation. Some common examples are given by Faraday (1974), who suggests some of the colloquial meanings that these images may represent. Several examples of the following have arisen in the course of the work of Robyn and myself.

- **Falling:** A common experience in dreams is that of falling from a great height: maybe falling off the edge of a cliff or building, or rolling down a hill. The metaphorical meaning could be about falling in someone's estimation, falling down on a job, or even falling in love. It is the dreamer's personal meaning that is the most relevant.
- **Flying:** This is another common dream scenario and could represent feelings of mastery, of feeling emotionally elevated, or of being in a 'higher' spiritual or religious state and so on. Alternatively, flying in a dream might be a representation of trying to escape, or flying away from something unpleasant.
- **Teeth falling out:** Although this is commonly associated with a repression of aggressive wishes, there are many other metaphoric meanings. 'No teeth' is commonly used in the sense that a pact or agreement cannot be made to 'bite' (i.e. has no potency) but it might also represent a 'loss of face' (i.e. a spoiled or marred self-image). Loss of teeth could also represent growing up, as indicated by the loss of baby teeth, or growing old.
- **Nudity:** Nudity or partial nudity in a dream often indicates a fear of exposure, or a wish for exposure in some important area of life. Being 'caught with one's trousers down' may indicate a lack of preparedness or fear of being made a laughing stock. A bare chest or breast may relate to a fear or desire to reveal an intimate thought or secret. Running naked down the street could be about a desire to be more open and honest in one's life or a wish to be seen for oneself.

- **Examinations:** Dreams of examinations are also common. These may represent being put to the test in some area of one's life or needing to prove oneself. They may also represent failing to pass some kind of test or not managing to live up to another's expectations.
- **Death:** It is important to consider the possibility of this theme as having a metaphorical meaning, since dreams of death are so frequently reported, and people often attribute sinister or frightening meanings to such dreams. Often people believe that dreams of death are predictive, hence they can cause a state of general anxiety and alarm. Another common belief is that a dream of death represents the dreamer's death wish for somebody, hence causing a state of intense anxiety and guilt. While not particularly subscribing to a theory of the predictive power of dreams, it is possible to acknowledge that the accounts that have been given very occasionally lend support to such an interpretation. The handling of this issue in therapy with dreams is discussed further in Chapter 9. However, in the first instance, clients are encouraged to look for plausible interpretations, and the search for the metaphoric meaning of death in a dream has usually proved to be very fruitful. Most frequently the author has found that it represents the closure of one chapter or relationship in a person's life, generally occurring at the point when that person is hesitantly exploring something new. Often, dreaming of death is a metaphor for leaving childhood dependency on parents behind, and assuming a greater degree of independence. Although this is a common meaning in the dreams of teenagers leaving home for the first time, it can apply to dreams of death at any age. Another metaphorical meaning found in death dreams can be 'done to death', indicating that the dreamer has had enough of a particular feature of their current life.

The range of metaphors is too great for an exhaustive description here but other examples can be found in Ann Faraday's book, *The Dream Game* (1974). It is worth pointing out that metaphors are not always the more common ones just described. An example of a more personal use of metaphor was found in one of Robyn's dreams.

> She dreamed that she was moving into a larger house which she was going to share with a female friend. The house was in Coventry. The meaning of the dream was not at first clear, but since Robyn had no waking associations or residue to link Coventry to her current life, the possibility that it had a metaphoric meaning was suggested. Immediately the phrase 'being sent to Coventry' came to mind. It became clear to Robyn that moving into a larger house with a female friend replicated her situation at work, where she was required to move into a larger office to be shared by a female colleague. The new office was located at a great distance from other members of her department. Robyn then realized that she had been harbouring a great deal of resentment concerning this move, and she was able to be more explicit about this when she realized that the move felt for her like being 'sent to Coventry', that is, out of direct communication with other members of her department. She subsequently took action to deal with her resentment, although she was not able to prevent the move.

Puns

The pun is another figure of speech that can play an important role in helping us to interpret dreams. Puns are very common in dreams and can provide powerful images. They can also be very amusing and can put the dreamer in touch with the creative and witty aspects of oneself, which may not always be apparent in waking life. Puns can be verbal or visual, or both. An example of a verbal and visual pun was found in one of Erika's dreams.

Erika had a dream concerning her place of work in which all her colleagues went off into the building in one direction whilst she went in another direction, which led her out through the front door of the office. She found herself standing in a street in her home town, which had somehow been transformed into a Middle Eastern setting. The ground was sandy, the pace of everything had slowed down and most of the people were in Arab dress. Erika knew that she was in Iran. Working through her dream, Erika found that most of the associations had to do with her thoughts about making a career change. However, the Middle Eastern setting made no sense at all. This dream took place before the recent conflicts in that region and all the events leading up to them, and Erika had no connection with this part of the world. When she was invited to give her dream a title, she unhesitatingly said 'Iran', and this immediately struck her as 'I ran'. She laughed at the obvious connection which she had now made with the work situation she was contemplating leaving.

Role reversal

As was outlined in Chapter 2, Jung believed that the characters in our dreams represent hidden or unacknowledged parts of the self. Thus the 'I' in the dream, also known as the 'dream ego', is often acting out an aspect of ourselves that we deny in our everyday lives. Perls went further and suggested that every single dream character or dream object represents a disowned aspect of the self. He suggested that by recognizing these disowned aspects and re-owning them we move towards integration and wholeness. In order to do most of this work we need to move into the process of Gestalt dialoguing, which will be described in Chapter 5. However, in an objective interpretive sense, this role-reversal aspect can come to the fore, particularly when the dream ego itself is represented in an unusual or atypical manner, or is seen behaving uncharacteristically.

Shaun, a successful, middle-aged advertising agent, dreamed that he was a young and apprehensive child, exploring his childhood home. Sam, a male art therapist, dreamed that he was a beautiful young woman taking part in a fertility dance, whereas Coral, a rather self-effacing young social worker, dreamed that she was dressed in tribal dress and wearing war paint as she confronted and drove away hordes of wild animals.

In each of these three cases the dreamer recognized, when working with his or her dream in therapy, that the dream ego represented a hidden part of themselves. Therefore each dream representation can reveal hidden parts of ourselves that we either do not consciously experience, or fail to reveal in our outward 'persona'.

Dissimilation

Dissimilation allows us to have some distance or protection from full recognition of a certain character in our dream. Often in dreams we have a sense of who a character might be, although we do not actually recognize him or her. The character might be someone we know, but thinly disguised, with one or more salient features changed, for example, hair colouring or altered physique. Sometimes we do not actually 'see' the person at all, but merely sense his presence.

> Alan described in detail a dream of a car journey through France. Although he said 'we' on a number of occasions when recounting the dream, he was apparently alone in the dream. Questioned about this at a relatively late stage in the interpretation, Alan eventually said that his wife was travelling with him in the car, although he sensed her presence rather than actually saw her. The presence of his wife in the dream gave an important clue to understanding the dream. Initially, all Alan's associations had been in connection with holidays in France, which were a regular occurrence for him. But the process of interpretation was sluggish and low-key and did not seem to be making any meaningful connections for him. Once he recognized his wife's presence, however, his associations began to relate to hospitals, and the tempo and level of energy rose. Alan began making connections to his own anxiety concerning a serious hospital operation that his wife was shortly due to undergo. Considering the nature of this event and the level of anxiety it aroused, it is perhaps not surprising that, even in the dream, Alan was distancing himself from the situation by this process of knowing that his wife was there, but not actually seeing her.

Fusion and transformation

Fusion means that two or more images come together in one compounded character or object. The results are sometimes bizarre but also imaginative.

> In Ann's dream, she appeared with a briefcase and dressed in high heels and a short, tight skirt. However, she was also wearing a nursing bra and was carrying a baby in a sling. The briefcase contained nappies and other items of baby equipment. At this time in her life Ann did not have children, but this image highlighted some of the conflict she was feeling over the issue.

In transformation, as the name suggests, an image is transformed into something else.

> In Kurt's dream the baby he was pushing in a pram turned into a large boulder which he was unable to move. For Kurt these images represented a change of attitudes from his pride in his new baby to a feeling of being held down by responsibility.

Omission

It is always worth checking in a dream to see if somebody or something is conspicuously absent from a familiar scenario. This can be an important piece of symbolism, and it is useful to try to find out the reason for the absence.

> Jill reported a dream that took place at the end of a training course that she had attended. Preparations were going ahead for an elaborate end-of-course party. When working on the dream, Jill's central focus was the absence of the second tutor from the dream, and how he had never properly understood or helped her on the course.

It is useful for therapists to have a working knowledge of the dream language and mechanisms that have been outlined so that they can make the dream seem less confusing or nonsensical to their clients. However, it is easy to get carried away with imaginative discoveries and detective work when attempting to translate the language of dreams. It is vital to remember that *the dream is only correctly interpreted when it feels right to the dreamer*. Dream interpretation is neither about being clever with other people's dreams, nor about imposing 'standard' interpretations on personal material. Therapists can make invaluable and insightful suggestions, but they are only suggestions and should be offered in a tentative way, allowing dreamers to find their own meanings to their own dreams. Some of the principles of interpreting dream language have been described before embarking on a detailed description of therapy approaches and methods, since they are particularly relevant when using the objective techniques that will be described in the next chapter.

Summary

In this chapter some of the important principles of dream language and cognitions have been outlined, since they are a necessary prequel to the discussion of 'objective' approaches in the next chapter. Whereas Freud emphasized symbols as concealing the latent content of dreams as well as their universal nature and meaning, Jung highlighted the revealing aspects of symbols and emphasized the more personal and changing nature of symbols. Some contemporary approaches to dream language include the cognitive approach as well as those of Weiss and Faraday. The cognitive approach considers that the dream needs to be understood in terms of the idiosyncratic themes of the dreamer's life, rather than in symbolic terms, and Ann Faraday's approach considers levels of interpretation to be important. Some mechanisms of dream language include: symbols dramatization; condensation and dilation; metaphors and puns.

4

Objective Approaches to Working with Dreams

In this chapter a group of techniques called 'objective methods' are described. Robyn Sewell and I classified the techniques we used into two broad categories, which we originally labelled 'objective' and 'subjective' approaches. The objective approaches are those which stay most closely with the dream scenario as it is recalled by the client. In order to examine the meaning of as many dream symbols as possible, it is necessary for the dreamer to disentangle themselves from the feelings associated with the dream, and comment on the dream from an objective, or outsider's, perspective. It is only after the symbols have been 'interpreted' or 'explored' as far as possible that the emotional aspects are re-integrated. These methods contrast with the more subjective and constructivist approaches of Gestalt and other methods, in which the dreamer is encouraged to re-enter the dream and to explore the metaphorical, subjective and affective experiences. In subjective and constructivist methods the dream itself becomes the starting point for the work, but the dreamer may then use the dream material in a variety of ways. These might involve following emotional and intuitive leads and allowing creative scenarios to emerge which may take the dreamer well away from the actual dream in an imaginative way. These subjective and constructivist techniques will be described in the next chapter.

Often objective methods are most helpful for longer dreams with a definite storyline. Some dreams may have complicated and action-packed stories with several scenes and many characters, and objective methods can provide the counsellor and dreamer with the tools to begin to unravel the complexity of such dreams. It is suggested that dream snippets, perhaps involving only sensations, may best be amplified using subjective and constructivist methods, but this is not invariably the case. Many dreams contain unusual or bizarre images or symbols which may appal or frighten the client. In these cases objective techniques may allow the dreamer to separate out, and distance themselves from, the dramatic impact and emotions of the dream sufficiently to be able to work out the dream meaning and message. The emotions can then be integrated at a later stage.

Some dreamers, who tend towards being more logical and intellectual, rather than emotional and creative, often prefer objective methods; they may find the more subjective methods too involving and overwhelming. However, there are no hard and fast rules about when to use which approaches. Clients who seem somewhat detached from the emotional content of the dream may find that subjective and constructivist methods encourage and facilitate them to access the dream affect. As was indicated earlier, the dream belongs to the dreamer and interpretation is a collaborative effort between therapist and client. Although a therapist's experience might lead them to suggest that a particular set of techniques might be most helpful for a particular dream, the dreamer's ability and willingness to work with the different methods is a crucial factor. Therefore, the choice of method depends on both the type of dream and the disposition and preferences of the client. The therapist's ability and willingness to work with the different approaches should also be taken into account. Therapists should not attempt to work with methods with which they don't feel competent.

The methods described in this chapter include ideas developed from Ann Faraday (1974), Lillie Weiss (1986) and Strephon Kaplan Williams (1984). While these methods may all be loosely termed 'cognitive', a more classical cognitive method, based on the work of Freeman and White (2002) and Hackmann et al. (2011), is also outlined.

Recounting a dream in stages

This sequence of steps is based on the work of Ann Faraday (1974) and Lillie Weiss (1986), and developed by Robyn Sewell and myself. The procedure provides a structure by which the therapist can facilitate the dream interpretation. The method is helpful for narrative dreams with several characters or objects. Although 'recounting a dream' can be used very successfully on dreams with only one scene, it is particularly helpful for dreams which have a long complicated storyline or several scenes.

Steps for the therapist to follow when working with recounting a dream in stages

1 The therapist begins by asking the dreamer to recount the dream in the third person, present tense. The dreamer is encouraged to concentrate on what the dream ego is doing. The dream ego is the person from whose point of view the dream is told. Generally this is the main actor in the dream, but occasionally the dreamer is an observer, in which case the dream ego is observing.

(Continued)

(Continued)

2 The therapist asks the dreamer to summarize the sequences in the dream substituting the word 'someone' or 'something' for every person or object in the story. Only the verbs remain unchanged. The example that follows these steps will help to clarify this process. This substitution highlights the actions of the dream ego while deliberately distancing the dreamer from other aspects of the dream. The dreamer often finds this procedure difficult and the therapist can help by modelling the process for the dreamer.

3 The therapist helps the dreamer to identify and note the feelings associated with each of the dream sequences.

4 The therapist then asks the dreamer to return to each action or scene and note the meanings of any people or objects. The therapist may find it helpful to ask the dreamer the following questions, although they do not have to be followed slavishly:

   a What does … mean to you? (The therapist inserts the name of the dream character or object.)

   b Are there any specific names, actual words, numbers or colours in the dream?

   c Can you recognize any metaphors or puns that emerge as you recount the dream? (Here the therapist can mention any that she or he has noticed.)

   d Are there any bizarre, paradoxical or contrasting images?

   e What are the main issues, conflicts or unresolved situations?

   f Are there any positive symbols, relations or resolutions?

5 The therapist then asks the dreamer to describe the major theme of the dream that has emerged.

6 The therapist asks the dreamer to give their dream a title. Here the therapist encourages the dreamer to say the first spontaneous title that comes into their head, since this is less likely to be subject to conscious censorship.

7 The therapist then asks the dreamer what the message of the dream is, that is, what the dream is telling the dreamer about their waking life.

8 Last, the therapist asks the dreamer what decision or action they can make in their daily life in order to actualize the dream.

The therapist should make notes of what the dreamer says at each stage, so that the therapist and client can consider the dreamwork that has taken place. It is also helpful to have a record of the dreamwork so that themes, symbols and so on can be compared to those appearing in later dreams.

EXAMPLE

First, Robyn asked Paul to recount his dream in the third person:

The dreamer is in a family kitchen with his wife and two other people. It's a pleasant atmosphere and they are preparing a meal. The dreamer notices a large beetle, like a scarab or bug, under the table. The bug starts to move and the dreamer decides to deal with it. He smashes it with the heel of his shoe and it breaks into several pieces. Each piece begins to reform into another bug and they each start to move. For a time the dreamer tries to hit all the bugs, but each time he hits them they turn into more bugs and become more active. Eventually the dreamer gathers up all the bugs and puts them into a coffee grinder in order to grind them up. As he grinds the bugs down finely, they turn into a green liquid. The dreamer carries the liquid over to a stainless steel shiny sink and pours it down the plug hole. As the green liquid goes down the sink it begins to become more granular again. The grains get larger and begin to form themselves into bugs again. At this point the dreamer decides that it's time to escape with the other people. In the next scene the dreamer is walking outside through a green, leafy, sunny glade with his wife. He begins to become aware of being separated from his wife and feels a sense of danger and foreboding. The dreamer attempts to try to find his wife and starts to run, with a sense of panic, through the wood. As he runs he becomes aware of the green bugs on the leaves of the trees overhead. As they grow larger, they begin to drop off the trees. Although he tries to avoid them, he is aware that bugs are dropping onto his back. The dreamer can't feel the bugs but he's aware that they are on his head. The dreamer becomes aware that the bugs have gone through his skull and are gnawing and eating away inside his head. The dreamer is aware that he is going to die and then he does die.

At this stage Paul said that, in the dream, he wasn't sure if he was dead or not. He became lucid and was aware that he was dreaming and woke up with some relief. Incidentally, it is often the case that people experience lucidity just before they wake themselves up from an anxious dream.

Second, Robyn asked Paul to summarize the sequences in his dream, substituting the words 'someone' or 'something' for each person and object:

Someone is somewhere pleasant with some people. Some people are preparing something to share. Someone notices something under something. Something starts to move and someone hits something. Something breaks up and reforms into some more things. Someone tries to hit all the things, but the things keep turning into more things and get more active. Someone eventually gathers up some things and puts them into something to grind them up. Something gets ground down into green something and someone carries the green something somewhere and tries to get rid of it by pouring it away down something. As someone tries to get rid of something, the something starts to reform again into the original things. Someone then decides to escape with some other people. Someone is then walking through a pleasant green something with someone else. At this point someone becomes aware of being separated from someone and feels a sense of danger and foreboding. Someone then tries to find someone and starts to run, panicking. Someone becomes aware of the original things hanging from some things above. Some things grow larger and

(Continued)

(Continued)

begin to drop onto the back of someone. Some things begin to gnaw and eat away at someone. Someone becomes aware that someone is going to die. Someone dies.

Third, Robyn asked Paul what feelings were associated with each of the sequences. Paul said that initially, in the kitchen with his wife and other people, he felt happy and content. Then he felt annoyance at the bugs and decided to kill them. As the bugs reformed in the sink Paul said he felt scared and in danger, with a sense of foreboding. When he decided to escape he felt relief. Paul then said he felt contented walking with his wife in the green, sunny glade. As he became separated he felt a sense of anxiety and urgency to bridge the gap. Paul reported that he felt scared and panicky as he tried to find his wife. He was aware of the danger to himself and his wife. As he noticed the bugs he felt increasingly frightened and had a sense of foreboding. Paul said he was terrified at his knowledge that he was going to die. After he had died in the dream, Paul said that, when he became lucid and woke up, he felt a sense of relief.

Robyn pointed out to Paul the repetition of a sequence of feelings that occurred twice in the dream. This was a feeling of contentment, followed by a sense of annoyance. This was followed by a feeling of anxiety and sense of danger and foreboding. This was followed by increased fear and, finally a sense of relief. This awareness of repetition of a sequence of feelings helped Paul to link the two parts of his dream.

As a fourth stage Robyn and Paul began to tease out the meaning of some of the main symbols in the dream. Associations to green fluid included life force, disinfectant and semen with sperm moving. At this point Paul revealed that his wife had become pregnant with their first child. Paul's interpretation of the rest of the dream stemmed from this link. Paul then became aware that he recognized the two people who had been in the kitchen as a couple with whom he and his wife had been friendly. Paul said that, when this couple had a child, the relationship between the couples had become more distanced. The child had somehow caused Paul to feel excluded by his friends. Robyn and Paul then worked on associations to the 'bug'. Associations to 'scarab' and 'beetle' were not particularly productive to Paul. However, he had an immediate association when Robyn suggested the metaphor of 'being bugged' by something. Paul immediately said that he felt a sense of annoyance or 'being bugged' by his friends' baby. Green seemed a prominent colour throughout the dream and the suggestion of 'life force' or 'nature' had led Paul into his exploration of the impact of children on his relationship with his friends. He did not immediately follow up Robyn's suggestion of green being also the colour of envy and jealousy.

Robyn continued by asking Paul about paradoxes or contrasts in the dream. Paul mentioned the secure, happy feeling when he was originally in the kitchen with his wife and friends when there were no bugs, and also the same feelings when he was in the glade with his wife before he became aware of the bugs. He contrasted these feelings with the feelings of foreboding and danger at the presence of the bugs. He also contrasted the association of green, natural, pleasant things with the green unpleasant liquid. Paul said that an issue or conflict that was unresolved for him in this dream was his separation from his wife. Another issue was that, the more he tried to kill or get rid of the bugs, the more they increased in size and number. He added that the issue of death in his dream was unresolved for him. In terms of positive relationships or resolutions, Paul said that the happy feeling of being with his wife, his energy to hunt for her when he became separated, and his decisiveness in acting to try to get rid of the bugs, were all positive aspects of the dream.

Turning to the fifth and sixth stages, Paul described the major theme of the dream that had emerged for him as being taken over by things, which will eat away at you and kill you if you don't deal with them. His spontaneous title for the dream was 'Green stuff'.

In terms of his waking life, and the seventh stage, Paul said that the dream was about impending fatherhood. The dream had highlighted his fears of the impact of a child on his relationship with his wife. He said that the separation from his wife and the death had made him aware how frightened he was that his wife would exclude him, as his friends had excluded him, when the child was born. Paul added that he had in fact felt a little jealous of his friends' baby and also that he was aware that he might feel a little jealous of his own baby if his wife excluded him after the birth. Paul said the dream had also made him aware of how important it was to deal with his feelings about this before they began to eat away at his relationship with his wife. Finally, at the eighth stage, in terms of actualizing the dream, Paul decided that he was going to deal with his feelings by acknowledging his fears and talking them over with his wife.

Some time later Paul reported that he had talked over his feelings with his wife. He had been a little anxious about doing this in case his wife felt that he didn't want the baby. In fact Paul's acknowledgement of his fearful feelings allowed his wife also to own up to some feelings of ambivalence, which she had been worried about revealing to him. The overall outcome of their talks was to bring the couple closer to each other. As well as sharing their fears about parenthood, they were also able to share their happiness and delight. Paul mentioned to his friends that, while he realized and understood the pressures of parenthood, he had missed their company. The couple acknowledged that having a child had somewhat isolated them. They, too, were anxious that the friendship would continue. This allowed the couples to acknowledge their feelings and to have a more realistic view of what was possible while their children were babies.

Readers will probably find other symbols and meanings in this dream. What is important, however, is that the therapist sticks to the associations and meanings that make sense to the client at the time. In this dreamwork, Paul initially rejected Robyn's association of the colour green with envy and jealousy. She did not, therefore, pursue this line. In fact, in this particular case, Paul did later own to having some jealous feelings. Robyn's earlier mention of the association of green with jealousy may have brought to Paul's attention feelings of which he was only dimly aware. Alternatively, it may have given Paul permission to acknowledge feelings of which he was somewhat ashamed.

Objectifying a dream

This method is a very slightly adapted version of the method of the same name outlined by Strephon Kaplan Williams in his book *The Dreamwork Manual* (1984). It consists of a series of questions which, like the previous method, provides an ordered process of dream interpretation for the therapist to follow. However, this method attempts to draw out meanings by suggesting a conceptual framework which highlights and clarifies aspects of the dream as well as helping the dreamer to integrate the dream, in a holistic way, into their ongoing experience. Experience suggests that this method can usually be completed more quickly than 'recounting the stages', although the time taken depends, to some extent, on the length and complexity of the dream. This method is not quite as thorough as 'recounting the stages' in that the latter method requires the dreamer to explore all the details of the dream in a fairly methodical manner. Objectifying a dream is probably better for therapists and clients who have had some experience of working with dreams, since the questions implicitly rely on a background understanding of a Jungian philosophy. Both methods can be used on the same kind of material, so clients can be shown both methods and let choose which they prefer. However, it is suggested that therapists experiment with both methods and work out their own preferences.

Steps for the therapist to follow when working with objectifying a dream

1 The therapist asks the client to tell the dream in the first person, present tense.
2 The therapist asks the dreamer to recount, in the third person, what the dream ego is doing and not doing in the dream. This concentrates the dreamer on the actions, or lack of them, in the dream.
3 The therapist then asks the dreamer the following questions, explaining them if necessary:
   • What are the major contrasts and similarities in the dream, and how do they relate to each other?
   • What sequences are in the dream, if any?
   • What are the major symbols, and what are the relationships between symbols?
   • What are the issues, conflicts and unresolved situations in the dream?
   • What are the positive symbols, resolutions or relations in the dream?
   • What relationship does anything in this dream have to any other thing in other dreams?
   • What are the possibilities for relationships and resolutions which have not yet materialized in this dream?
   • How would you summarize the particular character or identity of this dream?
   • What have you learned from this dream so far?

EXAMPLE

First, Rachel, a woman of mature years, told her dream in the first person, present tense:

> I'm in a big store trying to find my way out. The store changes into a big park and I'm still trying to find the exit. I see narrow gaps in some iron railings and I'm trying to find the right exit, but I'm not clear where it is. I'm trying to find my way; I know that I need to come out on the west side. But then I realize that, if I come out on the west, I'll be too near to Richmond and I need to be near North London. It's all right if I come out of the wrong exit because I'll be near Baker Street, which is familiar. I think I'm coming out on the west side; in fact I come out on the east. There is a road going north and also a smaller street going west, which I know will eventually take me where I want to go. There is a one-way sign, and I'm not sure from which direction it's one way. I see a car going in and I think it's OK. I turn into the one way street and, although I can't see where it's going, I know it will lead me in the right direction. Then I come to another park, which has narrow railings round it, and a gate which is too narrow to drive through. I get out of the car and walk. The park rises steeply uphill. There are railings on my left, and formal gardens on the right. I can also see a tearoom. I feel a tremendous strain on my legs and I'm anxious and think I have done too much driving. I think that I must make sure I keep my mobility. At the top of the hill there are some teenage children, hanging about. I vaguely seem to know them. Now I'm at the top I realize that I have to go back and get the car. I decide to go back a different way and I walk across the front of the tearoom and down some steps. The children point them out to me. That's the end of the dream.

Second, Delia asked Rachel what the dream ego was doing in the dream:

> The dream ego is trying to find her way home. She is driving a car and trying to find the right exit. She is not really lost; whichever exit she takes, she can get home. She turns up a one-way street, although she's not sure if she can go up it. Even though she can't see where the road is leading, she knows it's the right way. She reaches a small park and tries to drive in but the gate is too narrow. She parks the car and decides to walk. She climbs up the steep hill and feels that it's heavy going on her legs. She's worried about her health and resolves that she must keep herself mobile. She reaches the top and sees the children. She realizes that she can't get home on foot and decides to fetch the car in order to get home.

Delia then prompted Rachel to tell her what the dream ego was not doing in the dream. Rachel added:

> The dream ego is not finding the direct way home. She's not able to drive through the narrow gates. She's not asking the way or asking anybody for help. She's not communicating or interacting.

(Continued)

(Continued)

Third, Delia asked Rachel about similarities and contrasts in the dream. Rachel said that there was a similarity between trying to leave the first park with its narrow railings and the gates being too narrow in the second park. The similarity was in things being too narrow to get through. Rachel contrasted driving and walking. She said that she was more mobile when driving but that she couldn't get everywhere by car. However, when she was walking, she could get everywhere, but she had a problem moving. Rachel also contrasted being sure of the way with not being sure of the way. Thus, although she was uncertain of the direction, she knew that she would get there.

Rachel listed the sequences in her dream as: getting out of the park; trying to find the right way; becoming aware that it wasn't difficult to find the right way; hesitating about the one way street; moving along the one way street and feeling confident; reaching the park and not being able to drive in; leaving the car and walking; struggling uphill; reaching the top; realizing that she needed the car for the rest of the trip; and last, deciding to go back for the car.

The following is a list of Rachel's dream symbols and their meanings:

Parks:	Pleasant places; pleasant stages on a journey; difficulty in finding my way in and out of pleasant places.
Railings:	Represent a clear boundary; don't always see clearly where to go through them and whether other people can go through them; not clear where they begin and end.
Entrances and exits:	Obsession with coming in and out; also coming out heading in the right direction.
Car:	Something to move around in; can't complete the journey without it; life energy.
One-way street:	No turning back; a commitment to continuing to the end of the street.
Richmond:	Place where I was an unhappy teenager; going 'west'; want a direction that will go north and not west; an attempt to come to terms with something in my past; trying not to repeat the past.
Baker Street:	My way home; familiar territory.

At this point in the dream Rachel suddenly realized that the journey in the dream replicated a real journey she had taken the previous week. She had been leaving a course she had been running with her friend. She had dropped her friend off at Euston Station and continued home on her own. From this point on, the dream began to take a clear shape for Rachel. It is often the case that the dreamer has a sudden revelation in the course of the dreamwork. Even if this occurs, it is a good idea not to abandon the dreamwork at that point; completing the dreamwork may give further insights. Rachel then carried on with her list of symbols:

Terraces:	Neat gardens; order.
Flowers:	Pleasant; Spring.

Teenagers:	Friends have teenage children; contrast between modern teenage years and my teenage years.
Tearoom:	Solid; respectable; place to take refuge if necessary.
Steps:	A straightforward way of getting back to my car; represents that there is an easy way, it's not such an impossible journey.
Pain in legs:	Retirement; getting seized-up; need to do exercise.

Delia then asked Rachel about the conflicts and unresolved situations in her dream. Rachel said that she still hadn't got home in her dream. She added that there was a conflict about not having found the most direct exit to take her where she wanted to go.

When asked about the positive symbols in her dream, Rachel responded very positively. She listed: 'The confidence of knowing I can get there; overcoming the uncertainty and making the commitment of going up the one way street; having the choice between driving and walking; and the possibility of going back and getting what I want.' Rachel then added in a rather surprised way: 'And the teenagers: They showed me it was all right to go back and get something. They pointed the way to going back and recovering the positive parts of my own adolescence.'

At this point Rachel was not able to see any connection between anything in this dream and any of her previous dreams.

Delia then asked Rachel what were the possibilities for resolutions that had not materialized in the dream. Rachel said that there was a possibility that she could have somebody alongside her offering positive help and pointing out the direction. She added that she could also use a map.

Delia then asked Rachel to summarize the particular character of this dream. Rachel commented that she thought that the dream was about circumventing obstacles on her journey. She said that the dream pointed out to her that she knew her destination but was having problems finding her way. She added that it was surprising and reassuring to her that she knew where she was going.

Finally, Delia asked Rachel what she had learned from the dream, to which Rachel responded: 'I may need to do some going back in order to go forwards. I have to deal with the Richmond stuff – my teenage years. If I do deal with it, it will help me to go where I want to go. The truth is that I have been there so many times and I have to go back there again.'

In discussion, Rachel said that she had been surprised to learn that she could trust her instinct that she did actually know where she was going. She had been surprised by the certainty of that knowledge in her dream. Rachel said that it had been about two-thirds of the way into the work before she realized what the dream was about. She had thought the dream might be about an impending career change until she had connected up Baker Street with a journey that she had actually made the previous week with her friend. She had been talking over her own teenage years with the friend's teenage children. She remembered that the dream had in fact occurred when she was staying at her friend's house. Rachel was not new to counselling and had been in therapy several times before. However, she realized that she had still more issues to resolve over her own rather unhappy teenage years. Thus, the dream pointed out to her the important issues, which she subsequently worked on in future therapy sessions.

Key questions

The method known as 'key questions' has been adapted from a method described by Strephon Kaplan Williams in *The Dreamwork Manual* (1984). 'Key questions' consists of a series of questions which the therapist can help the dreamer to apply to their dream. There are obvious similarities between this method and the previous two approaches discussed in the chapter. However, this method does not necessarily require the dreamer to work their way systematically through the dream, but allows them to choose to respond to questions that seem interesting or relevant. It can be used with the same kinds of dream material as are suitable for the other objective methods, but is perhaps particularly helpful when the dream seems rather confused, with no clear storyline, or when the dream is only partially remembered. Some dreamers may already have some idea of what their dream is about and may just respond to certain key questions in order to clarify particular issues.

Steps for the therapist to follow when working with key questions

The therapist should initially ask the dreamer to tell the dream in the first person. The choice of tense is not particularly important with this method, although the present tense is usually preferred, since it brings the dream to mind more vividly for the dreamer.

The therapist can give the dreamer a copy of the list of key questions. She then instructs the dreamer that they are free to respond to as many of the questions as they choose. Clearly, not all the questions are relevant to every dream. The therapist suggests to the dreamer that they choose questions which create the strongest feelings within them. Therefore, the dreamer is encouraged to choose the questions that they are either drawn to positively, or those which they consciously wish to avoid. It is often the case that those questions that the dreamer shies away from may relate to important issues. The list of questions is:

1 How are you, as dream ego, acting in this dream?
2 What symbols in this dream are important to you?
3 What are the various feelings in the dream?
4 What are the various actions in the dream?
5 Who or what is the adversary in the dream?
6 Who or what is the helping or healing force in this dream?
7 What does this dream suggest that you are avoiding?
8 What does this dream suggest is being healed in you?
9 What questions does this dream ask of you?
10 What does this dream want of you?
11 Why did you dream this particular dream now?
12 What relation does this dream have to anything that is happening in your life?
13 What actions might this dream be suggesting that you consider?

---

14 Why did you need this dream?
15 Why are you not dealing with the situation in this new way?
16 Why are you not doing this in your life?
17 Where are the helpers and guides in your dream, and in your life?
18 What choices can you make as a result of working with this dream?
19 What is being accepted in this dream?
20 What can happen if you work actively with this dream?
21 What new questions come up from this dreamwork?

EXAMPLE

In this example, a dream has been chosen in which the dreamer attempted to answer all the questions. However, it is rarely the case that all the questions are seen as relevant. Mary is a single, professionally successful woman aged 39. She dreamed this dream shortly after the break-up of a recent love relationship. At the time she was feeling very unhappy. Delia asked Mary to tell her dream:

I was in a large store, like Lewis's. I was alone in a fitting room trying on a suit with a purple, checked, pleated skirt. The skirt reminded me of one I had as a girl. I couldn't make up my mind whether to buy the suit. I looked at myself in the mirror. The jacket buttoned up to the neck and the skirt was long. I checked to see if the suit was a bargain. But I wasn't sure, there were three price labels on the jacket. I couldn't see what the original price was; the other two labels had £9.70 and £9.90 on them. I decided to buy the suit but, before I changed, I decided to see if the jacket looked better with the high collar undone. I undid the buttons, I was naked underneath and all I saw was a bony chest. It looked bad. I decided I definitely needed a black polo-neck sweater to cover myself. I took the suit out to the woman shop assistant and noticed that she'd changed to go home. I realized that the shop was closing and all the other people had gone. I asked her how she would like me to pay for the suit, and offered to pay by Visa card. She looked doubtful so I offered her a cheque. This seemed worse; she said that Visa was better. I went out into the street carrying the suit in a bag. In the street I took the jacket out of its bag. Then I saw that the jacket was more brown than purple, though it did have a purple line through it which matched the skirt. I realized that, although the two items did go fairly well together, I had not got a suit. I immediately thought how clever shop assistants were to find a way to display garments which went together, so that people would buy them. In the middle of this scene I had a flash of another part of the store, which was the toy department. A man customer was buying a big board game from a boy assistant. The boy who was serving the man offered to show him how to set out all the pieces. But the man replied that his grandmother played the game a lot, and she would show him how to play.

(Continued)

(Continued)

Delia then asked Mary to respond to as many of the key questions (see Box above) as she cared to:

1   Mary said that, as the dream ego, she was acting as she normally would, looking for bargains and being rather undecided about buying.
2   Mary then listed the symbols and the meanings she associated to them:

Purple skirt:	Skirt her mother made when she was a girl; personal ability to choose. Mary added that she had just remembered that she had an argument with her mother, who had wanted Mary to have the skirt long, whereas Mary wanted to have it much shorter, above her knees.
Long skirt:	Keeping sexuality covered.
Suit:	Matching of two separate parts.
Bargain:	Something that is just right. Mary added that she shouldn't be looking for something that was just right.
Unbuttoning jacket:	Can I open up sexually?
Black polo-neck sweater:	Concealment; cover up.
Shop assistant:	Mother. Mary suddenly realized at this point the association with her parents who had owned a shop, where she had been brought up and spent all her childhood years.
Shop:	Home life; relationship.
Board game:	Rules of the relationship game.
Man:	Men in general; a potential partner.
Boy serving the man:	Things are not as you expect them to be.
Grandmother playing children's game:	Everything is topsy-turvy.

3   Mary described her main feeling in this dream as confusion. She was confused about whether to buy the suit, and said that this reflected her waking confusion over the rules of the relationship game. Like the sale of the board game, these rules seemed topsy-turvy. Mary added that she felt annoyed when she got outside the shop and discovered that she did not have a suit but only matching garments. She also felt admiration for shop assistants who could pick out matching things and make them work.

4   Mary described the various actions in the dream as looking at herself in the mirror, unbuttoning the jacket, offering to pay and accepting what she had got.

5   Mary said there was no major adversary in the dream, only her struggle with herself. She did acknowledge, however, that the shop assistant was making life difficult for her.

6   Mary said that she was the healing force in the dream. She said that her recognition of the mismatch and her acceptance of the garments as being nice, anyway, was also healing. The skirt and jacket were OK. They just didn't make up a suit.

7   Mary said that she thought that the dream was suggesting that she was avoiding close relationships. Although she opened up the jacket, she decided that she needed to cover up with a black polo-neck sweater.

8   Mary thought that the dream was an attempt to heal herself from a relationship that had broken down.

9   Mary thought the dream was asking her why she had to cover herself up, and why she had to go back to long skirts.

10 Mary said that she thought the dream wanted her to stop looking for bargains, i.e. things that were just right.

11 Mary thought she had dreamed this now because her relationship had just broken down and her conflict over close relationships was very much at the forefront of her mind.

12 Mary said that she thought that the mismatch in the dream was similar to the mismatch that had occurred in her life.

13 In terms of the actions the dream might be wanting her to consider, Mary thought that the dream might be telling her to 'button up', and not to 'open up'. However, she thought that the dream might want her to accept and like things that were less than perfect, or flawed in some way.

14 Mary said that she thought that she needed this dream in order to help her to feel better: 'It showed me that I can accept that things just don't match, but it doesn't make it any less worthwhile.'

15 However, Mary said that she was unable to deal with the situation in this way because deep down she still believed there was a perfect match.

16 In terms of her life, Mary said that she was still torn between buttoning up and looking for a compromise.

17 In answer to this question concerning the whereabouts of Mary's guides and helpers in her dream as well as in her life, Mary initially said that the assistant was a helper. However, when Delia questioned Mary about this, Mary said that the shop assistant didn't help her because she 'rushed her through and wasn't very facilitating'. Mary pointed out that there were no real helpers in her dream; those people who might have helped her in fact didn't help her. Mary said that she felt alone in her dream and alone in her life.

18 Mary felt that the choices that she could make as a result of the dream were to 'button up' and not risk revealing herself in relationships, or to accept a compromise.

(Continued)

(Continued)

19 In reply to the question about what she is accepting in her dream, Mary said she thought that she was accepting that compromise is OK. She thought that things could be nice even if they weren't made for each other.

20 In order to work actively with the dream, Mary thought she needed to work more on the issue of whether and how to be involved in relationships.

This question is intended to stimulate discussion about the dreamwork. Mary discussed arguing with her mother over the length of the skirt and also mentioned the row, many years ago, when her mother had discovered Mary's contraceptive pills. Since her parents were often busy in their shop, Mary didn't feel that they had enough time for her. Delia reminded Mary about the shop assistant, whose job was to help, but who 'rushed her through, and wasn't very facilitating'. When discussing her childhood, Mary said that she never knew if she was doing the right thing, or even whether she was wanted. As a child she was not sure if she should go into the shop; often when she did go in, she was told to go away because her parents were busy. Mary felt that this had led her to feel rather insecure about close personal relationships.

In her present life, Mary said that she felt that she didn't have some of the necessary skills for close personal relationships in that, as illustrated by her dream, she didn't know what the rules were, what the real price was, and what was the correct way to pay. Mary felt that the choices were to open herself up or not to allow herself to get involved in close personal relationships. It seemed hard for her to find a balance between the two pole positions. Other aspects of the dream that Mary commented on were the fact that it was closing time in the shop and that she felt she had to make her choice quickly. This may have been a reference to age and the fact that she would be 40 in a few months time. In the dream Mary was satisfied with the compromise, but she was also aware that she would have liked the outfit to be a proper suit. When Delia asked her to focus on the end part of the dream, Mary said that she was aware that she was satisfied with the compromise. She also said that the garments were 'wrapped up'. Delia commented that Mary was carrying the bag with her in the street and wondered if this might be 'baggage' that she was carrying around with her. Mary then commented on dream aspects that she had not previously mentioned: at the end of the dream, she was on her way home and it was sunny; and that suits were not her style anyway.

This dream is packed with rich symbols and metaphors, and readers may well find issues that have not been drawn out in the above dreamwork [question 21]. In such a rich dream as this, it is often difficult to deal with every aspect, and it is suggested that the therapist might help the dreamer to distil those aspects which are of immediate importance. The dream can always be worked on again at a later stage. This dream illustrated some classic dream mechanisms: the skirt and the shop served to set the context of the dream by linking Mary's unhappy feelings about current relationships with childhood feelings and relationships. Another interesting aspect to this dream was that it was operating at several levels. Indeed, Mary herself moved between these levels in her interpretations. At one level the dream was about Mary's feelings concerning her relationship with her mother as well as her feelings about the relationship in her current life that had broken down. At another level, the dream may also have been about aspects of Mary that were not absolutely 'suited'. In the sense in which the suit may also have represented herself, does Mary have to be 'perfect' or is she good enough as she is? Although Mary's mother might have wanted her to have a suit, Mary also knows that this isn't her style, and maybe she is 'nice enough anyway, and worthwhile'.

Cognitive method

This classical cognitive method has been outlined by Freeman and White (2002) and summarized by Hackmann et al. (2011). The steps below are slightly adapted from these workers. A dream analysis record (DAR), which is a dream reporting form designed by Freeman and White (2002), is also shown at the end of this section.

Steps for the therapist to follow when working with a cognitive method

1 The therapist asks the client for a dream analysis record (DAR). (See below for an example of this, which is similar to a dysfunctional thought record). This might have been done as homework or can be completed in the session.
2 The dream is described and the cognitive themes are explored. The thematic content of the dream is idiosyncratic to the dreamer and needs to be viewed within the context of the dreamer's life so that the meaning of a particular dream experience needs to be understood in terms of the client's overall view of life.
3 There is reflection on and linking to how these themes are also manifest during waking life.
4 The client considers how they would like to feel about the dream and how they would like to behave differently in the dream (and by extension in life).
5 In imagery the client experiments with changing the dream in various ways.
6 The client continues until they have found an acceptable and believable alternative that they feel better about. The client might then rehearse the new dream by writing the new version down or repeating it several times.
7 The client then reflects on what this means in terms of their waking life and how they might experiment by responding differently to similar situations in the future.

When working cognitively with dreams an assumption is made that clients will be encouraged to change their dreams. As already noted, cognitive therapists consider that dream themes directly reflect clients' waking thoughts, concerns and schema. Since clients are working in cognitive therapy to restructure these negative thoughts in more positive and adaptive ways, it follows that therapists will encourage clients to change their negative dream images to more positive ones. Some of the principles of working with nightmares are therefore relevant here. In general and where they want to change a negative aspect of the dream, clients should be encouraged to be active rather than passive, to confront rather than to avoid, to be powerful rather than reacting and to say something that wasn't said in the original dream. It is important that the therapist reflects the strong and/or negative feelings that the dream may engender, without trying to minimize these. However, an important aspect is to encourage and empower the dreamer to find ways of overcoming these through their own resources.

EXAMPLE

Sophie is a 28-year-old counselling doctoral student who struggled to complete her assignments on time. As the time of a deadline drew near she would begin to panic and would often wake up sweating with a feeling of terror. Her current recurring anxiety dream, which she had had since school, albeit in slightly different forms, was of being in a large examination room doing a statistics exam when two male professors in black academic gowns descend on her and tell her that she isn't meant to be here and evict her from the exam. In therapy Sophie quickly identified her waking cognitions as: 'I'm not good enough'; 'I'm bound to fail'; 'I shouldn't be here (at university)'; and 'I'm worthless'. As part of her therapy, which included anxiety management and cognitive restructuring, Delia asked Sophie to restructure her dream. Initially Sophie found this hard and couldn't think how she could act differently in her dream; in her first attempt she hid from the men. But with help from Delia she began to create a different scenario whereby when the two men appeared and asked her to leave, Sophie rose to her feet and confronted the men, telling them that she was a bonafide and extremely capable student and that they should leave. The men leave and Sophie completes the exam. As Sophie became more empowered and began to become more assertive and take control by confronting the men in her dream, her feelings changed from anxiety to relief. She began to feel more confident and capable in her life and was able to approach her assignments with more equanimity. This was helped by the good feedback that Sophie obtained from her tutors.

Dream analysis record (DAR)

The dream analysis record (DAR) is a method for recording dreams and the associated cognitive work designed by Freeman and White (2002) and also recommended by Hackmann et al. (2011). A slightly adapted form is presented in Figure 4.1.

Figure 4.1   Dream analysis record (DAR)

Date	Dream report	Degree of emotion (0–100)	Dream restructuring	Re-rate emotion (0–100)

(From *Oxford Guide to Imagery in Cognitive Therapy* by Ann Hackmann, James Bennett-Levy and Emily Holmes (2011); Figure 10.1 'Dream Analysis Record', p.141, Chapter 10. Reproduced by Permission of Oxford University Press)

Summary

Objective methods are essentially those that stay most closely with the dream story as it is reported by the client. The dreamers attempt to disentangle themselves from the feelings associated with the dream and to work on the dream from an objective, or outsider's, perspective. 'Recounting a dream in stages' presents a series of steps for the therapist and client to work on the detail of the dream narrative. 'Objectifying a dream' similarly provides an ordered series of steps, though the method utilizes a Jungian conceptual framework to highlight and clarify aspects of the dream. This is followed by 'Key questions', which allows the dreamer to respond to questions that seem interesting or relevant rather than necessarily working through the dream systematically. Finally, a classical cognitive method of dream interpretation is presented. This takes the therapist and client through a method for recalling and restructuring negative dream themes through changing the negative imagery in the therapy context.

5

Subjective and Constructivist Approaches to Working with Dreams

In this chapter are described some ways of working that are grouped together under the heading of 'subjective' and 'constructivist' approaches. There is, of course, inevitably some overlap between these methods and those described in the previous chapter. However, these approaches tend to be intuitive rather than analytical and they almost invariably put the dreamer in touch with the 'feeling' content of the dream. When using these approaches therapists will usually be encouraging clients to enter into the metaphorical, subjective and affective experiences in their dreams, which is consistent with the constructivist perspective in psychotherapy. The emotional impact can be quite strong and often the insight may closely follow the emotional expression. Subjective approaches may involve bringing the dream to life in the 'here and now' and can involve a reworking or adaptation of the dream material. Hence it is possible for the process to move quite a long way from the content of the dream into the direct or imaginative experience of the client.

These methods often involve the client getting 'inside' the emotional content of the dream and are more likely to lead to a greater personal awareness than to some form of prescription for action. The insights gained generally concern internal conflicts within the person or the dreamer's feelings about others in his or her life, rather than action or interaction with the environment. This is because, with subjective and constructivist approaches, the emphasis is on the linkage with the qualitative or feeling aspects of the dream rather than on the symbolic or story-telling aspects. Thus, these methods will generally be most helpful for interpreting dreams at level two ('through the looking glass') and level three ('looking inward'), according to Faraday's schema of interpretation described in Chapter 2. Level two interpretations concern the dreamer's reactions to people and situations, whereas level three interpretations concern conflicts within the self. As has been indicated earlier, the method chosen also has to be compatible with the client. Sometimes people are happier working at the symbolic, rather more intellectual, level and are diffident with the subjective approaches. Other clients will work readily with these methods.

It is hard to give specific indications about what kinds of material these methods work best with, but dreams where only snippets are remembered, or which have very strong visual images, are generally indicated. These methods can work well where people have a very intense emotional involvement with their dream, or with people who are able to move imaginatively forward and/or who can respond readily in an uncensored and natural way. They are not indicated for people who have had any kind of psychotic episode or whose grip on reality is very tenuous. These methods can be very dramatic and are often more powerful in a group. Although they can be used as self-help methods, they are not easy to do by oneself. In fact, the methods themselves usually call for at least one other person. They may take people into very personal material in depth and therefore the therapist needs to allow the client real choice and options for stopping. It is important to respect these therapeutic safeguards. Often, quite a lot of experience is necessary before a therapist will be comfortable using some of these methods.

A step-by-step guide to each method will be outlined, followed by examples and some practical hints for usage.

Gestalt method of dreamwork

Steps for the therapist to follow when working with Gestalt

1 The therapist encourages the dreamer to recount the dream from the start, in the present tense, and in the first person.
2 The therapist helps the dreamer to speak as the main elements of the dream. The dreamer should choose those characters or objects:
   a about which they are most curious or uncertain
   b about which they have the most powerful feelings
   c which are noticeable by their absence from the dream.
   It is important not to focus entirely on characters in the dream but to work with any element, whether an inanimate object, animal or abstract entity. In each case the dreamer should describe themselves as 'I', tell the dream from the point of view of that element, and say how they feel about the other characters and objects in the dream.
3 The therapist then helps the dreamer to develop a dialogue between any characters or elements. It is important for the dreamer to physically change places to a different chair or cushion when he speaks as a different element. This physical separation of each dream element onto a separate chair helps to emphasize the separation of the dream elements and to avoid confusion. In order to develop a dialogue, the dreamer and therapist might:

---

a   look for potential conflicts and explore them

b   look for blockages and try to move them on

c   allow various dream images to speak for themselves until a 'topdog' and an 'underdog' emerge.

As outlined in Chapter 2, the dialogue between the 'topdog' and the 'underdog' will often develop into a quarrel which will give information about the nature of the conflict, usually internal, underlying the dream. Perls believed that the nature of the 'underdog' will give the client information about something in waking life that is being avoided and which needs to be recognized.

4   The therapist should support the dreamer to make the 'underdog' stand up to the 'topdog' and state their needs. This provides the existential message of the dream.

5   The dreamer can continue with this method of dialoguing, referred to in Gestalt work as 'hot-seat' work, in order to explore any issue the dream has brought up.

6   The therapist helps the dreamer to consider what the dream tells them about the way they live life now, and what kinds of changes they might wish to make. When attempting to sum up the dream, Perls believed that it is helpful for the dreamer to consider what is the 'existential message' of the dream as well as what, if anything, is being avoided in the dream.

7   The method of feedback and group sharing by which the dreamer's personal work is reviewed is very much a part of the Gestalt technique.

That it is done in an appropriate manner is important in individual work and absolutely essential in groupwork. The suggestions that follow apply to the therapist in individual work and to the therapist and other group members in groupwork. A full example of group feedback can be found in Chapter 8.

8   With Gestalt, as well as with other techniques, it is important, during feedback, to stick to what is noticed or felt during the session. It is not considered valuable for the therapist to interpret, give advice or force their views onto the dreamer. It is more helpful for the therapist to attempt to identify with some aspect of the work and share their feelings or experiences. The person who is giving feedback should take responsibility for their own feelings and views in such a way that it allows the dreamer to take on board any parts that are helpful and reject the rest. The therapist can encourage the use of a feedback format such as 'When you did ... I noticed ...' or 'when you said ... I felt...'. It is mostly not helpful to question the dreamer about why they did things in a certain way. Often questions are a way of avoiding taking responsibility for making statements.

EXAMPLE

Dupinder recounted her dream in the first person, present tense:

> I'm standing inside a small house by the sea, which is surrounded by a small garden on four sides with a fence all around it. As I look at the beach the waves are getting bigger and bigger and are breaking over the garden of my house. Now a huge wave, in a giant arc, breaks over my house. I can see that

(Continued)

(Continued)

the fence around the garden is beginning to break up. Although I'm feeling quite exhilarated by the waves, I'm also quite frightened. Now I'm getting more frightened that the waves are going to break up my house.

Dupinder then spoke as various elements in the dream:

As the wave: I'm strong and powerful. Nothing can stop me. I am pure energy and I can move mountains. I'm going to get bigger and bigger and sweep this house away.

As the house: I'm a fairly small house, simple and straightforward. But I'm quite a nice house; I'm comfortable and cosy. I like the excitement of the big waves, but now I'm frightened that I'll be swamped by them.

When Dupinder spoke 'as the house' an expression of understanding appeared on her face. She explained that she identified herself with the house in her dream. The experience of being a wave related to the feelings evoked by the recent relationship in which she had become involved. She enjoyed this relationship but was beginning to feel encroached upon and that her individuality was being restricted. Dupinder explained that she and her boyfriend had recently started living together.

Robyn suggested that Dupinder carry out a dialogue between the house and the wave in her dream. In summary:

As the house: I want you to keep sweeping over my garden and encircling me; I admire your strength and beauty. But I'm a bit afraid of you. I don't want to be drowned by you.

As the wave: I am strong and powerful and I enjoy my power. But I don't want to destroy you. I'd better recognize that I mustn't overpower you. You may be simple but you stand on solid ground and I want you to stay there. So I'll slow down and lap gently around you.

As the house: I want you to stay and I will reinforce my fence with stones so that I'm less fragile and not so easy to wash away.

Dupinder breathed a sigh of relief and smiled broadly. Perls suggested that when an integration or resolution takes place it is accompanied by an emotional release. This can be a strong release of emotion or a slight sign, such as a sigh or a smile. This gives an indication to the therapist that this may be a good point to stop the dialogue. Robyn asked Dupinder if this was a good place to stop, and Dupinder confirmed that this was the case. Dupinder explained that the message of the dream to her was that she needed to maintain her own position and recognize her own strength within the relationship.

In her feedback Robyn commented to Dupinder that she had noticed how strong Dupinder's voice had sounded when she was speaking as the wave and how hesitant and quiet she had sounded when initially speaking as the house. Robyn reminded Dupinder how, as the house, her voice had become more energetic and decisive as the dialogue had progressed. Dupinder said that this reflected how she, as the house, had felt more positive and able to state her point of view. She went on to explain how she had been avoiding tackling issues that had come up in case they had risked the relationship. She now recognized that if she didn't speak up then the relationship wouldn't work anyway. Dupinder later reported that, as a result of the dreamwork, she had discussed her feelings about the relationship with her partner. This had resulted in her feeling more comfortable and positive within the relationship.

The therapist can facilitate the process and encourage the person to stay in the first person, present tense by gently correcting the language of the dreamer. For example, the therapist can insert 'is' to bring the work back into the present if the dreamer slips into using 'was'. They can help the dreamer to clarify the process by making sure they move physically each time they speak as a different element in a dialogue. They can also remind the dreamer, when they change chairs, what the previous element said, using the same words whenever possible. They can offer support by staying in close proximity with the client as they change chairs. Sometimes, the judicial use of touch, such as a hand on the shoulder, can be helpful; at other times this can inhibit the client. It is important for the therapist to use their feelings to stay closely in touch with the client. Often a particular statement, maybe a feeling or an existential message, will resonate with the therapist, who can echo the words and ask the dreamer to repeat and amplify the words. The technique can appear directive, so it is important for the therapist to offer their suggestions as experiments that the dreamer is free to try out or reject. If the dreamer repeats and exaggerates particular phrases they can see whether or not emotional energy resides in them. Sometimes it may be clear to the therapist that the person is avoiding saying particular words and may say 'Can I offer you a sentence?' or 'Try these words to see if they fit'.

In a dreamwork session where John was dialoguing with his father, who had died some time previously and who frequently appeared in John's dreams, it appeared clear to Delia that the words John was avoiding saying were 'I really loved you, Dad'. When Delia suggested he try these words, John burst into tears as he said the words he had not been able to say in life. Of course, the words John wanted to say might have been 'I never really loved you, Dad'; it wouldn't have mattered if Delia had suggested the wrong words because John could have corrected her. Alternatively, John could have actually said the opposite words, which may have made him more aware of what he really wanted to say. One technique of Gestalt is to work with resistance rather than against it. If John had found it difficult to say 'I really loved you, Dad', Delia might have suggested he say the opposite words, thus going along with John's resistance. If John had then acted on Delia's suggestion, he would have felt his resistance increasing and, paradoxically, reached the point where he really wanted to say the opposite words.

In attempting to work with Gestalt the therapist should try to stay where the energy or awareness is for the client in the dream. So questions like 'What are you most curious about?', 'Which part of the dream has most energy for you?' can help put the dreamer back on track. It is important for the therapist to observe closely the client's body language and non-verbal gestures or movements. By directing the client's attention to these, the therapist can help the client to keep in touch with the emotional energy of the dream. In John's case, Delia noticed that his hands were in a praying position and she drew his attention to them by saying 'Are you aware what your hands are doing? What are they saying?'. John replied (as his hands) 'We are praying for John to be able to say what he wants, to his father.' Often the therapist will have no idea where the dreamer is going and should just attempt to stay closely in touch with the client and facilitate the process. Gestalt is based on the belief that the client really knows what is best for themselves and will take themselves where they need to go. The therapist should not attempt to impose a direction or worry unduly about resolving the issue. If the client appears stuck and/or the therapist does not know what is happening, then the therapist can ask 'What's going on for you?' or 'What's happening now?' and get some direction from the client.

Gestalt work is not as easy as it may appear and therapists are strongly advised to acquire some experience and confidence using the techniques before trying them out on clients. There are several places in Britain where Gestalt training is available. Useful books are: *Skills in Gestalt Counselling and Psychotherapy* (Joyce and Sills, 2010); *Gestalt Counselling in Action* (Clarkson, 2004); *Brief Gestalt Therapy* (Houston, 2003); and 'Reflective practice and humanistic psychology: The whole is more than the sum of the parts' (Cushway, 2010).

Hill's cognitive-experiential model of dream interpretation

Clara Hill's influential and integrative model (Hill, 1996, 2004) draws on a variety of theoretical models including humanistic, gestalt, psychoanalytic and behavioural approaches. However, she has chosen to focus on cognitive and experiential methods in her three-stage model, which involves exploration, insight and action. This model, as the name suggests, integrates an experiential with a cognitive approach, and is presented below in an adapted form from Hill and Rochlen (2004).

Steps for the therapist to follow when working with Hill's cognitive-experiential model

1 The therapist describes the model and gives the client a brief overview.
2 **Exploration stage**
   a The client recounts the dream in the first person, present tense.
   b The therapist asks the client about their feelings in the dream and on waking.
   c The therapist then uses the acronym DRAW (description, re-experiencing, association, waking life triggers) to explore each of the major images in turn. It is impractical to explore every image in detail, so it is helpful for the therapist to encourage the client to focus sequentially on the most important images whether they are objects, people, feelings or thoughts.
      • *Description* means asking the client to describe the first image in as much detail as possible.
      • *Re-experience* feelings. The therapist helps the client to focus on the feelings which make the image become more real. The therapist can use a variety of techniques such as reflection of feelings or exploring bodily sensations.
      • *Association* involves the therapist in encouraging the client to say what the particular image means to them. One way of facilitating this is for the therapist to use a technique developed by Weiss (1986) and ask 'What is ... for you?'. The therapist then tries to elicit more details about the meaning of the association for the client. Hill considers that this stage is crucial for enabling clients to access the cognitive schemas to help the therapist and client understand the dream.
      • *Waking life triggers* involves asking the client to think of waking life events that might be related to this particular dream image. (These may have emerged already.)
   d The therapist then summarises this exploration process by substituting images with descriptions, feelings, associations and waking life triggers.
3 **Insight stage**
   a The therapist then asks the client for their initial understanding of the dream. Depending on the client's level of understanding and whether or not they are happy with this, or whether they want to do more work on understanding the dream, the therapist can then collaborate with the client to construct a meaning for the dream on at least one level. It is important to remember that the dream is only correctly interpreted when it makes sense to the dreamer and, as discussed in Chapter 3, any dream can be interpreted or understood at many levels. Hill and Rochlen (2004) have described five levels that they consider relevant. I have found Faraday's levels two and three, described in Chapter 2, helpful. So the dream could be usefully explored at the following levels:
      • *Waking life:* Dreams typically reflect waking life concerns and most clients naturally explore this level first. Therefore the dream can be thought about in terms of current life and relationships.

(Continued)

(Continued)

- *Internal dynamics:* The dream can also be thought about in terms of intrapersonal issues or 'parts of the self'. This is similar to the Gestalt idea where each image/person in the dream is part of the client's personality.

b The client and therapist then summarise the meaning of the dream that they have arrived at.

4 **Action stage**

If the client is willing and ready, the therapist can help the client work on developing an action plan which might also involve the possibility of changing the dream.

a Ask the client to change the dream. This can be a creative way of getting the client to think about changes that they could make and it can also empower them to:

- Bridge to changes in waking life. Devise an action plan for ongoing development.
- Devise a ritual to 'honour' the dream. Some clients like the idea of marking the work they have done with a ritual or symbolic act.
- Help the client think about how to continue working on the dream. (This is optional.)
- Encourage the client to summarise their action plan.
- Ask the client to give their dream a title. (This is optional, but can be a good way of encapsulating the dreamwork that has been achieved.)

EXAMPLE

Helen recounted her dream:

> I'm with my husband and a woman comes up and tells us that the car, that we have spent a long time repairing and have just got back, has been crashed. I see the car, which has been completely written off. I'm completely shocked and devastated and get angry. My husband, Andy, seems less surprised and, as he is trying to comfort me, he says 'It's alright, I've got another car', which is a shiny red American car. I think 'Why didn't he tell me that before' and feel angry and a bit cheated. Then the scene shifts to a square, that I don't know, and Andy and I are sitting having coffee. One of my daughters lives near the square and I wonder whether to knock on the door and visit my grandson, Jack, or whether it is too soon, as I only saw him recently. I can't decide what to do. When I wake up I feel puzzled.

Having told the dream in the first person, present tense and explored the feelings, Delia and Helen entered the **exploration** stage and Helen chose three images to work on using the DRAW acronym. Helen first chooses the car image and describes it as looking completely scrunched and smaller than it was and with its front, sides and back all scrunched up with its roof caved in. Helen said she felt as if someone had punched her in the stomach and then was very angry. When comforted by Andy she felt a mixture of feelings, relieved but also as if she had been cheated out of her anger by his disclosure that he had another car. When asked to associate to this image, Helen immediately said 'I wonder if it's me'. She then said 'It's as if everything I try gets destroyed' and described recent events in her life where she had been making progress but where she had experienced setbacks which she felt had put her back to 'square one'. An example of this was her recent attempts to get fit and lose weight, which had been undermined by illness.

Helen chose, as her second image, to focus on her feeling of anger. As she focused on this feeling she associated it with her perennial struggles in her life to manage her feelings of anger. She sometimes felt conflicted in her relationship with her husband, which was generally positive and supportive, but at times felt irritated by Andy's wish to close down her anger prematurely since he was very uncomfortable with anger. As her third image, Helen chose the square; as she did so she suddenly became aware of the link between the two parts of the dream and described an incident where she had recently got angry with her daughter and had been supported by Andy in her reconciliation visit. Helen described the square as being somewhere in France, and she identified her feelings of wondering which course of action to take as similar to her efforts in life to achieve balance for herself. As an example Helen described her awareness of a need to balance her wish to achieve good marks in her university course with taking care of herself.

Helen was happy with the work she had done on her dream, and at the **insight** stage identified waking life issues in her family relationships connected to the way she managed and expressed her anger. However, Helen had also identified a meaning connected to her own internal dynamics when she had identified herself as the scrunched car in her dream. She had identified her feelings of being undermined and somewhat defeated by recent setbacks in the progress she had made in her life. From her dream sequence in the square Helen identified her quest for balance and harmony in her life. Unusually, she had found herself able to reflect and consider what to do without getting angry. This sequence was set in France, a foreign country. Delia reflected whether this was a recent and unusual place for Helen to find herself in.

At the **action** stage Helen felt ready to consider what changes she would have wished to make to the dream. She said that she would have wanted Andy to apologize and to allow her to express her feelings of anger before comforting her and presenting her with the new car. Immediately, Helen thought about how that could be a bridge to her waking life. She decided that she could have a conversation with Andy and tell him that she would like him to validate her feelings of anger before stepping in. She said that as 'he didn't do anger', maybe she could reassure him that her anger wouldn't damage him, and that if he could slow down a bit and hear and acknowledge her anger without closing it off prematurely, she would find that extremely helpful. She also thought that she would acknowledge how his support and comfort had allowed her to manage her feelings of anger with her daughter.

(Continued)

(Continued)

Helen thought she would look at how she could continue to reduce the pressure and stress on herself and achieve more balance in her life.

Helen thought that she would 'honour' her dream by drawing a sketch to symbolize the work she had done, and she called her dream 'the car crunch'. Clearly, there may be more work that could be done at a future stage, but Helen was able to find meanings for her dream at two levels and was satisfied with the work that she had done to date. It is important to remember that the dream is correctly interpreted when it makes sense to the dreamer. Helen is a skilled and self-aware dreamer who will undoubtedly continue to reflect on the meanings of her dream.

Kelly's constructivist approach to dreams

George Kelly, who was the founder of Personal Construct Psychotherapy, developed the idea of constructive alternatism. That is, while there is a true reality, reality is always experienced from one or other perspective, or alternative construction. There are in fact an infinite number of constructions we are able to take and, if the one we choose is not helpful or adaptive for us, we are able to put another construction on the world. So Kelly postulated that if reality is something that we create, our task is to help the client find ways of construing what is happening to them. In Kelly's view dreams represent the most loosened form of construing that that can be put into words. Therefore, since dreaming is a loosening activity, the content of a dream is less important than the 'telling' of a dream and its tone and feeling content; the dream can change in the course of its telling. With dreams it is more useful to be loose for longer because tightening narrows down meaning. The following exercise encourages clients to explore various meanings for their dream.

Steps for the therapist to follow when working with Kelly's constructivist approach

1 Write down the first and last sentence of a dream (Kelly suggests that the first sentence characterizes a dream and maybe says all that has to be said). The therapist encourages the client to say it with different inflexions and emphasizing different words.
2 Take one image or experience of telling the dream.
3 Write this in capital letters as if it is the title of something and underline it. Encourage the client to think what kind of thing this might be the title of.
4 Place it in the centre of a page and make associations to it.

5 For each association the therapist helps the client to think of as many questions around the association that they can.

6 The therapist then asks the client what they need to pay particular attention to in the work they have just done.

7 The therapist encourages the client to think of one small action that they can make in waking life to honour that dream (e.g. symbolic, practical, kinaesthetic – needs to be something physical).

EXAMPLE

This is a dream that the client, Joyce, worked on alone and in between therapy sessions. Joyce was a therapist herself and was used to working on her dreams. Delia talked Joyce through the steps and she was able to work through her dream on her own at home. In this case, although Joyce had a dream in mind, Delia never heard the whole dream but just the working through that Joyce brought to the next session.

1 First sentence: 'I awoke with a shock and realized that I had been dreaming.' Last sentence: 'And now I realize that the worrying about something is so much worse than the experiencing of it.'

2 Joyce took the image of 'panic' and made the following associations to it:

helpless

retirement   mother's death

health anxiety   PANIC   alone

not in control   feeling old

shock

3 Joyce brought to therapy her working around the association of 'retirement' which had the most resonance for her.

4 Joyce reflected on the following questions around 'retirement':
  • What is retirement? For Joyce this was something to be frightened about.
  • How does retirement make me feel? Joyce felt panicky and frightened.
  • What colour is retirement? Joyce thought the colour of retirement was black and to her this symbolized death.

5 Joyce decided that she needed to pay attention to her previously unacknowledged fears around retirement, which she was due to face within the next two years. Joyce decided that she wanted to make her existential fears a focus in her therapy.

6 Joyce decided to visit one of her, fairly recently retired, friends to discuss her thoughts about retirement.

This approach is interesting in that it is not even necessary for the client to bring to therapy, or even remember, the whole dream. The method, which utilizes the first and last sentence, encourages the client to create alternative constructions and meanings for their dream experience.

Dream re-entry

Re-entry is a method of working on the dream in the waking state. The dreamer closes their eyes, gets into a deeply relaxed state and visualizes a dream scene. The dreamer can imagine or visualize asking a particular question of the dream, or not, as he wishes. The process is then one of letting go and seeing what happens. This method has been borrowed from Strephon Kaplan Williams (1984), who uses a combination of Jungian and Senoi techniques, and it can be useful either when the dreamer wishes to get some resolution to some aspect of the dream or when the dream is unfinished and the dreamer wants to investigate what happens. A modification of this method can also be used when working with nightmares and it will be referred to later in the context of changing the story ending. There are several ways in which re-entry can be done: it can be done alone as a private meditative exercise, or it can be done with a facilitator in the form of guided re-entry. Some people are more able to relax and visualize when on their own, whereas others find that a facilitator or guide keeps them on track. We have found that, particularly when the dream is anxiety-provoking or frightening, a guide can be a support by enabling the person to re-enter the dream state. Although this method is called 're-entering a dream', it is of course attempting to recapture the atmosphere of the dream and then continuing it by daydreaming or fantasy. Often dreamers have felt that they are back in the dream and have experienced the associated emotions.

First is described how to work with guided re-entry, and then instructions for self re-entry are outlined. With self re-entry the role of the therapist is simply to provide the instructions to the dreamer to use this technique at a time and place of his choice and, afterwards, to facilitate a discussion of the experience with the dreamer.

Steps for the therapist to follow in working with guided re-entry

1　The dreamer recounts the dream in the first person, present tense.
2　The therapist or guide helps the dreamer to get into a relaxed state.
3　The therapist or guide then asks questions or gives suggestions to the dreamer. These will depend on what is appropriate but might include:
　　a　At what point would you like to re-enter the dream? Using the present tense, describe the scene in detail.

b   Is there anything you would like to change in your dream?

c   Now, just let the action continue, try not to censor and verbalize what is happening.

d   Would you like to make a different choice in your dream?

e   Do you need any help from anyone or anything?

f   Bring the helper into your dream and see what happens? (This question allows the dreamer to introduce some support in the form of a 'dream friend', an idea mentioned in Chapter 1.)

g   Are there any blocks? If so can you find a way of dealing with them?

h   Is there anything else you need to do in your dream?

i   Find a suitable stopping place.

j   Take your leave of your dream knowing you can return when you choose.

k   Slowly come back to reality and look around.

4   The therapist asks the dreamer if they would like to share and process the experience, but avoids analysing or interpreting the dreamer's experience.

5   The therapist asks the dreamer in what ways the dream is relevant to their waking life.

EXAMPLE

Martina described her dream:

I'm in a very large, old-fashioned house – rather like a stately home. I'm exploring the house and now I'm walking, in one wing of the house, along a long, dark and gloomy corridor. There are doors leading off from the corridor but they are all closed. I'm wearing an old-fashioned rich, heavy gown. It comes down to my ankles and I have ermine slippers on and a very high and elegant head-dress. I want to go forward but I'm afraid and feel too weighed down to move freely. All I can see is blackness. I push at a door but it won't open and I wake up.

Robyn: At what point would you like to enter the dream?

Martina: At the part where I'm walking along the corridor. I'm trying to walk along. These clothes don't allow me to move freely, I feel weighed down. I keep pushing at these doors but they won't open.

Robyn: Is there anything you want to change in your dream?

Martina: Yes. Now I can see some light at the end of the corridor and I'm going to move towards it. I'm getting a bit closer but I feel more and more weighed down.

Robyn: Do you need any help?

(Continued)

(Continued)

Martina: No; I'm almost there. Oh! now I can see there's an open archway in the wall at the end. I can see through the archway. There's a beautiful sunny cove, with a beach and deck chairs. There's a family playing on the beach. I think it's the beach I used to go to as a child. I want to go down there but I can't get through the archway!

Robyn: What's stopping you?

Martina: I'm weighed down by these clothes.

Robyn: Can you find a way of dealing with the problem?

Martina: I can take my cloak off. I'm taking my cloak and slippers off, but I'm still stuck.

Robyn: Do you still want to go through the archway?

Martina: Yes, but I'm too heavy; my head feels weighed down.

Robyn: Is there anything else you can do?

Martina: Yes, I think I'll take my head-dress off.

As she made this suggestion Martina went through the physical act of lifting the heavy head-dress off. As she did so her expression changed; her face lightened and she smiled, lifted her head up and said 'I can go through now'. Martina then described herself on the beach with the family, feeling free to play and splash around in the water. She stayed in a radiant state for a minute or two. Then Robyn invited her to leave her dream, reminding Martina that she could return to the dream whenever she chose. Martina explained that the clothes in the dream represented respectability and conformity. She said that in many ways she was yearning to throw off some of the yokes in everyday life, many of which were self-imposed. Martina said she had always felt a need to conform but that the dream had given her a glimpse of wider horizons and that she was going to find ways to feel freer in her life.

Steps for the therapist to instruct the dreamer in self re-entry

1 Write down your dream and then see what questions or issues are suggested by the dream and its imagery. There may be situations which seem unresolved or you may wish to continue the dream story, or an aspect of it, to see what happens.
2 Choose the questions or situations you most wish to deal with and write down your question or intention.
3 Have either a tape recorder or paper and pencil with which to record the results.
4 Find a comfortable place where you will not be interrupted and prepare by using your preferred method of relaxation.

5 Relax and visualize the dream scene. Remembering your question or intention, let go and allow the action and images of the dream to develop. Without attempting to analyse or censor, see how the imaginative dream process develops.
6 Continue until you choose to stop or feel that a natural resolution has occurred.
7 Write or record your experience, and then process your results.
8 Consider how your experience relates to the questions or intention you started with.
9 Finally, consider what relevance the dreamwork has for your waking life.

EXAMPLE

Annette chose to use this method on another dream from her 'hospital series', from which another example in Chapter 8 is also taken. In this dream:

Annette was told that her friend, Jim, had been involved in an accident and been taken to hospital. She rushed down to the hospital and was told that she could not see her friend yet, she would have to wait. After waiting for what seemed to her like a long time, Annette again asked if she could see Jim; again she did not get a satisfactory answer. Feeling frustrated, Annette set off to look for her friend. She went past a room; she looked in and saw a face she did not recognize inside a freezer. Annette then went on through two closed doors and found a tall upright fridge with a glass door. Standing in the fridge was Jim. He seemed to be put together out of pieces, half of which were human and half made out of plastic, resembling an android. Annette knew that Jim was alive. However, when she opened the fridge door Jim was unable to talk to her. Annette then went to ask what was wrong with Jim, but none of the nurses or doctors would answer her questions.

Annette was dissatisfied by this dream. The main issues she wanted to resolve were, why nobody would tell her what was happening, and why her friend was in pieces. Annette, who is a strong visualizer, settled down, relaxed, and imagined the dream scene. The following is the account that Annette wrote immediately after the dream re-entry:

I went through the dream until I had found Jim. I thought that he was alive, but actually he didn't seem really alive or dead. He seemed sort of suspended. So I went and found a nurse who had previously been unhelpful. I asked her why my friend was in a fridge and why he was in pieces. She said: 'We can't mend him, there's nothing more that we can do. We haven't got the technology yet. We can mend some of the bits. But then all we can do is freeze him and wait until we are able to mend him.' I knew then that this dream was about HIV and AIDS and I wanted to tell the doctors and nurses that they should communicate more about what is going on. I found a small

(Continued)

(Continued)

group and said to them: 'You have to tell people what's going on. Even if you can't tell them very much, you should tell them what you know and not leave them in the dark.' They told me that they would but that they felt helpless. The most that they could do was to mend the bits that they could and then freeze people until they could put all the pieces back together, putting real bits back instead of plastic pieces. At this point I felt that I knew why my friend was in pieces, that I had made some sense of my dream, and that I felt safe to leave it there.

Self re-entry can be done entirely alone. Alternatively, it can be carried out in the presence of a therapist, if this feels safer. Guided re-entry can be done individually, with a therapist/guide and dreamer, or in a group setting. In the latter case the group members can take the dreamer's dream on board and work with it as if it were their own. At the end other people can share their experiences, but without attempting to analyse or interpret the actual dreamer's experience. The dreamer may find aspects of other people's experiences relevant to their own and can give feedback about this if they wish. A similar, but more structured, exercise is given in Chapter 8.

The role of the guide in guided re-entry is neither forcing a direction nor just listening and reflecting. The guide should be sensitive and supportive, possibly suggesting a direction but always emphasizing that the dreamer has free choice and should not push themselves into areas that are too frightening or overwhelming. Providing the dreamer is not pushed, they will naturally protect themselves from becoming too overwhelmed by the re-entry. One difficulty could be that the dreamer may get stuck in the same conflict as in the original dream. In this case the guide might ask the dreamer how they might deal with the conflict and what help and resources they need to deal with it, possibly suggesting alternative directions.

Summary

Subjective and constructivist approaches encourage dreamers to enter experientially the metaphorical, subjective and affective experiences in their dreams. This is consistent with the constructivist perspective in psychotherapy. Working through a dream from a Gestalt perspective, which utilizes the first person and present tense, is followed by Clara Hill's cognitive-experiential model of dream interpretation. In this method clients are encouraged to combine experiential insight with more behavioural action planning. This is followed by an example of working from Kelly's constructionist perspective where the actual content of the dream is less important than the 'telling' of the dream. Finally, two forms of dream re-entry are described in which the client is helped to visualize and change a part of their dream.

6

Working with Nightmares

In this chapter nightmares and ways of working with them are discussed. First, the types of nightmares, their incidence and causation are briefly described. A discussion of some factors creating nightmare distress and ways of alleviating it is followed by an outline of some of the basic principles and methods for working with nightmares in both the waking and sleeping state.

Nightmares have been defined as 'frightening dreams that usually awaken the sleeper from REM sleep' (American Academy of Sleep Medicine, 2001). This description probably fits the experience of most of us who suffer from the occasional nightmare and wake up with a memory of frightening dreams. 'Anxiety dreams' are similar to nightmares in that people can become very anxious during horrible dreams and these are only distinguished from nightmares by the fact that the person normally fails to wake. There is another less common category of nightmare called a 'post-traumatic nightmare'. This is an aversive and recurring dream that repeats in sleep a negative experience that has actually happened in life. It almost invariably occurs after a trauma, such as involvement in a war or an accident, and the nightmare is not a fantasy but a re-experiencing of the actual event. It is one of the defining symptoms of post-traumatic stress disorder. The methods of intervention to be described in this chapter are not generally suitable for post-traumatic nightmares, which will be discussed in the next chapter.

Not so much is known about nightmares as is known about ordinary dreams, since they don't seem to occur under laboratory conditions. Ernest Hartmann, in his book *The Nightmare* (1984), has concluded from his investigations that, although nightmares can be a symptom of psychological disturbance, they are not necessarily a pathological symptom. In fact, he found that frequent nightmares may occur in relatively healthy but sensitive people. He suggests that nearly everyone will have an occasional nightmare, particularly under stress. About 50 per cent of adults will remember occasional nightmares, whereas 5 to 10 per cent of adults will report regular nightmares. The greatest incidence of nightmare reporting is in young children, and between 10 per cent and 50 per cent of the population will suffer between the ages of three and six. Thereafter the incidence of nightmare reporting decreases with age. Although more women report having nightmares, the incidence is not necessarily higher; it is possible that women may be more willing than men to admit to them. Nightmares increase with certain illnesses and stressful periods, as well as with certain medications. There is some evidence that certain personality characteristics, particularly schizotypal personality, but also borderline personality disorders, schizoid personality disorder or schizophrenia, are associated with the presence of frequent nightmares (American Academy of Sleep Medicine, 2001).

Most nightmare themes involve feeling helpless in the face of threat. In adult nightmares the basic fears are often the same as those in childhood, such as fear of loss or fear of retaliation for a hostile wish. Many of these basic fears re-occur at times throughout our life and can precipitate nightmares in the adult. Most nightmares occur latish in the night and often towards morning when periods of REM sleep are longer. There is speculative evidence that in the earlier periods of sleep, when REM periods are shorter, our dreams are more straightforward and contain more day residue. As we move through the night we may be processing earlier and earlier material and this is the time when childhood anxieties are more likely to be evoked. Most nightmare themes, then, involve experiencing a state of absolute helplessness. Surveys have shown that common nightmare themes for both adults and children include being chased or attacked, being injured or dying, being paralysed, sensing something scary (without attack) or falling. Common themes for anxiety dreams include taking an exam, arriving too late, being frustrated, or appearing nude or wrongly dressed in public.

As mentioned earlier, increased frequency of nightmares may be related to certain medications, in particular L-dopa and related drugs as well as beta-adrenergic blockers. There is no evidence to support common myths that nightmares are actually caused by gastric disturbances, oxygen deprivation, nicotine, cheese or chocolate. However, if sleep is disturbed by any of these, there is an increased probability of the sleeper waking during an REM period, and hence remembering more dreams. There is also evidence that withdrawal from certain substances, notably alcohol, barbiturates or benzodiazepines, all of which reduce REM sleep, can cause a REM rebound. We mentioned earlier that if we are deprived of REM sleep for any reason, we will make it up when we are allowed to sleep normally. This so-called 'REM rebound' effect can produce increased dreaming and, sometimes, intense nightmares. Some years ago Delia saw a client who had attempted to overdose on barbiturates. When the barbiturates had worked through the client's system, she began to experience horrifying nightmares. The frequency and severity of these nightmares suggest that they were probably caused by the REM rebound as the drugs wore off. Of course, it is also true that those people who are recovering from a suicide attempt will probably be suffering from a high degree of psychological distress and so may be prone to increased nightmares, but therapists should be aware of the REM rebound effect. Delia's client, although distressed, was somewhat reassured to learn that REM rebound was probably contributing to her nightmares. Indeed, the frequency and severity of her nightmares reduced rapidly within a few days. Therapists can be somewhat reassured that these days safer hypnotics, such as zolpidem and zaleplon, are normally prescribed. Therapists who would like more information about drugs can refer to a review of medications for the treatment of sleep disorders by Pagel and Parnes (2003).

Halliday (1987) discusses factors creating and alleviating nightmare distress, and reviews some psychological methods of dealing with them. He outlines four factors that lead to nightmare distress. First, many people believe nightmares to be important; in particular they are often thought to be prophetic. Second, nightmares usually do have an extremely anxiety-producing storyline; this can often be something that would be horrific to anyone, such as dreaming of being in a coffin, or it may be an individual horror such as a person with a phobia of dogs dreaming of dogs. Third, nightmares do seem very realistic; they seem much more upsetting than watching the same actions on television or at the cinema. Many of us will have had the experience of finding it difficult to shake the nightmare feelings off even when awake. It is a common experience to wake up and still be very frightened, perhaps imagining that the enemy or monster will come in through the doors or windows. Fourth, Halliday cites the perceived uncontrollability of nightmares as a factor leading to distress. Halliday comments that an intervention that can affect either the beliefs that nightmares are prophetic and uncontrollable, or the realism and ability of the nightmare to create anxiety, should have a positive effect on alleviating nightmare distress.

Increasing personal feelings of safety may help to reduce the fear of nightmares. It has been reported, although not empirically tested, that some people report more nightmares when they sleep alone than when someone else is in the room. This might be a relatively simple thing to change and may be worth a try, especially in the case of children. Simply telling the nightmare to a sympathetic other can often be helpful. It can allow the person to become more comfortable with the nightmare as well as helping to put it in perspective. Therefore, it is usually helpful to allow the person to talk about the nightmare; again, this is especially the case with children. Parents may attempt to reassure their child by telling them that their nightmare is not real. This is rarely helpful, and it is better to allow the child to talk about the nightmare and express their feelings. These suggestions are really common-sense measures.

Before attempting any more elaborate intervention it is recommended that an appropriate diagnostic screening be carried out to eliminate any psychological or physical disorders. One particularly important factor to be aware of is the possibility of physical and/or sexual abuse. Garfield (1986) has reported that nightmares may be the primary indicator of sexual abuse in children and the second most frequent indicator, after acting out, in adolescents. Garfield also suggests that the frequent occurrence of nightmares in adults can indicate the possibility of sexual abuse in childhood, even when this has not been admitted in therapy. The therapist should be alerted to the possibility of other symptoms, for example, significant childhood amnesia or psychogenic breathing difficulties, such as asthma, reflecting this kind of abuse. Obviously, where a psychological or physical cause for nightmares can be identified, this should be the focus of the intervention rather than the nightmare per se. The methods we are going to describe should only be used when identified causes have been addressed.

It is possible to work on nightmares in both the waking state and the sleeping state. Methods can be practised when the client is awake, either with a therapist or by the dreamers on their own, usually using written methods, guided fantasy or other imaginal techniques. The results can then be carried by the dreamer into the dreaming state using dream incubation to change their nightmare. Dream incubation is described in more detail in Chapters 1 and 9. A description of interventions using 'storyline alteration' and 'face and conquer' is followed by examples of the Gestalt method, which can be used very fruitfully with nightmares. Next, there is a discussion of 'lucid dreaming' methods whereby the nightmare intervention can be made while the dreamer is actually asleep and dreaming. Finally, principles and suggestions for working with children's nightmares, including a paperwork method, are outlined.

Storyline alteration methods

As its title suggests, this method provides ways in which the anxiety-producing storyline and/or its ending can be altered. Although this approach can be used in a variety of nightmare situations, it may be most helpful where the client is very fearful about the nightmare. In this case the client may be unwilling to attempt the 'face and conquer' method which, as its title implies, requires the dreamer to turn and face the feared object in her nightmare. The storyline alteration approach may also be used where the client and/or therapist are unable or unwilling to work with the Gestalt approach. If the client is very frightened, a relaxation technique used as an adjunct to the storyline alteration approach may desensitize the dreamer sufficiently to work with the nightmare.

Steps for the therapist working with storyline alteration

1 The therapist encourages the dreamer to repeat the dream first in the third person and then in the first person, present tense until they feel a little more comfortable and accepting of the nightmare.
2 The therapist and dreamer discuss what interpretation or meaning the dreamer gives to the nightmare.
3 The therapist asks the dreamer how they could change the storyline of the nightmare to make it less frightening. At this point the therapist helps the client to elicit appropriate changes. It may be necessary for the therapist to suggest alterations. However, the modification to the story should be one that the dreamer finds acceptable.
4 The therapist encourages the dreamer to run through and practice the new version of the story in their imagination.
5 When the dreamer is used to the nightmare in its new form, the therapist suggests that the dreamer should imagine, and thus re-experience, the new version of the nightmare while in a relaxed state before going to sleep.
6 The dreamer makes a suggestion or intention that the desired alteration will be incorporated into the nightmare, if it is experienced again when the dreamer is asleep. This last stage is essentially dream incubation, as was practiced by many ancient cultures. This is a suggestion or self-suggestion by the dreamer for a particular kind of dream.

EXAMPLE

Tony described a nightmare he had been having for several weeks in which he was standing at the top of a lift shaft and falling down past endless floors and lift gates. In the nightmare he fell forward and head-first down the lift shaft. The speed increased as he went down but he never reached the bottom; it was an endless journey. In the therapy session Tony explored his fear that, if he reached the bottom of the lift shaft in his nightmare, he would in fact die. This is a fairly common myth and Delia was able to give Tony many examples of people falling, reaching the bottom, dying and being dead in dreams, and still being alive to tell the tale! Tony said that the most frightening part of the nightmare was the rate at which he was falling and the fact that he was falling head-first. At this point Delia asked Tony what he thought the nightmare meant and asked him about the symbols and metaphors in the dream. She asked if there was any place in Tony's life where he was falling head-first. Tony said that, although he had not really acknowledged the fact, he was probably falling in love. Tony revealed that he had got involved with his best friend's partner and the situation was getting 'a bit out of hand'.

(Continued)

(Continued)

After discussing the situation in Tony's life, Delia asked Tony how he could change the dream to make it less frightening. Tony said that, if he went more slowly and could see where he was going, he wouldn't be so frightened. Tony decided that he would like to fall more slowly and with his feet first. He also thought that, if he held out his arms and made his hands bigger than they were in life, they would slow him down. He thought that in his dream he could then choose to visit various floors on the way down if he wanted to. Tony ran through his new version of the dream several times in the session and seemed visibly more relaxed. Delia explained steps 5 and 6 (see above) to Tony and suggested that he tried them out at home.

When Tony returned the following week he reported that he had not had the nightmare again. He said that he had suggested to himself that the story was altered along the lines they had discussed in the session. He dreamed that he was gliding down a wide, light shaft. He was able to see open doors on each side of the shaft and, by moving his arms, was able to direct and control his movement and pause and look in at various floors. Tony went on to talk about how he had decided to end his involvement with his friend's partner, although this would be difficult, and explored some of the implications that this decision would make to his life.

One way that the therapist can help the client who is experiencing nightmares is by normalizing the experience; that is, explaining that such bizarre and frightening dreams are relatively common and that they do not necessarily reflect some deeper pathology. Education can be reassuring, as in the case of Tony's dream, where Delia was able to explain that reaching the bottom of an abyss was a fairly common dream symbol and did not result in death. Information can also help to allay the commonly held fears that nightmares inevitably have a sinister prophetic connotation.

Modifications to the above steps are that the therapist can facilitate and rehearse the different story or ending, either by dream re-entry, a guided meditation sequence described in the previous chapter, or by re-writing the dream, which is described next. Another common alteration to the storyline is that the dreamer chooses a dream helper to give them support. This is a modification of the Native American system of a 'spirit guide', as described in Chapter 1. An example of calling on a 'dream friend' for support is given later in this chapter.

Re-writing the nightmare

Re-writing the nightmare is another form of storyline alteration which the therapist can do with the client in the session or, more usually, the client takes the instructions away and completes the exercise as homework. Whether the therapist chooses this method or the method of storyline alteration described above largely depends on the client. Some clients like writing between sessions and so would naturally prefer this approach. It can also be empowering for the client to do this on their own.

Steps for working with re-writing the nightmare

1 Recall a nightmare.
2 Summarise the nightmare. What is the dream ego (i.e. the dreamer) doing/feeling?
3 Choose which actions/attitudes are positive and/or valuable for you and which are negative for you.
4 Choose a point in the dream where you would like to change a negative aspect: As a dream ego you can change your involvement.
   • At a time of choice you can choose differently.
   • Choose to be active rather than passive.
   • Choose to confront rather than to avoid.
   • Choose to be powerful rather than reacting.
5 Sit comfortably with pen and paper.
6 Re-write the dream with the dream ego going through the same scenes but this time using the new, more creative attitudes. Let your words and feelings flow.
7 Read through the new dream scenario.
8 Make a new statement to summarize what the dream ego is doing/feeling.

Face-and-conquer methods

Face-and-conquer methods are based on what is known as the 'Senoi' system of dream control, where the dreamer is instructed to face or to confront and conquer the feared object during the dream. The Senoi were reported to be a tribe living on the Malaysian peninsula. Although their culture has apparently now been largely destroyed, their dreamwork was originally reported by an American psychologist called Kilton Stewart in a paper called 'Dream theory in Malaya' (1969). The tribe was also visited by the dreamworker Patricia Garfield, who describes their culture in her book *Creative Dreaming* (1974). This work draws heavily on her ideas. Generally, the Senoi worked with dreams in two ways: they worked to change the dream state while dreaming; and they did dreamwork projects using dream material to alter their lives for the better. In the Senoi tradition children were taught to stay in their dreams, even under scary conditions such as falling. They were also taught to experience the dream state as capable of being controlled. The Senoi methods can be a valuable way for people to confront their nightmare fears.

Since this method encourages the dreamer to confront their dream enemy, it can be helpful where the nightmare involves the dreamer being chased or attacked by a dream enemy, or where the dreamer senses a threatening presence of some sort. Some clients are more willing to use a guided fantasy method, such as the face-and-conquer method, than they are to work with the Gestalt approach. To some extent, then, the choice of method rests with the client's preferences as well as the competencies of the therapist, who may not be trained to use the Gestalt method. This method can also be used in conjunction with Gestalt, for example, to enable the dreamer to explore their nightmare attacker prior to working with the Gestalt method. The general principles for the Senoi system of dream control are:

1 Always confront and conquer danger in dreams.
2 Always move towards pleasurable experiences in dreams.
3 Always make your dream have a positive outcome and extract a creative product from it.

The following steps in Senoi dream control can be implemented in several ways. The dreamer can work through the method either in self re-entry or guided re-entry. The therapist can take the dreamer through the method as a form of guided fantasy, which is a method we have often used. Finally, the dreamer can use the approach while actually dreaming by becoming 'lucid' using the method to be described later in this chapter. The following steps are intended to be carried out in the waking state.

Steps for the therapist working with face-and-conquer methods

1 If the dreamer is the victim of any aggressive action or attack, they should become reciprocally aggressive.
  a The dreamer should attack the dream enemy.
  b The dreamer should fight, to the death if necessary:
    i The death of a dream enemy releases a positive force from the part of the dreamer that has formed the antagonistic dream image.
    ii The essence of the dream enemy that is killed will emerge as a helpful, positive figure for the dreamer.
  c The dreamer should call on a dream helper or helpers to help her, if needed, and meanwhile she should fight by herself until they arrive.
  d Any dream figure that is either aggressive or refuses to help is to be considered an enemy:
    i Figures that appear to be friends but attack or refuse to help are really enemies in the disguise of friends.
    ii Dream characters are enemies only so long as the dreamer is afraid of them. If the dream enemy is amorphous, rather than a specific image, the dreamer should also move towards it and see what happens. Often as they move towards an amorphous enemy in a dream it will change to something else, either negative or positive.
2 After the dreamer has confronted and subdued an aggressive dream image, they can force it to give them a gift.

---

a The gift can be something beautiful, such as a poem, a story, a design, a dance or a painting.
b The gift can be something useful, such as an invention or a solution to a problem.
c The dreamer should bargain only if necessary to get this gift.
d The gift should be one that is valuable to the dreamer in their waking life.
3 As in the storyline alteration method, the therapist can suggest to the dreamer that, prior to going to sleep, the dreamer should make a suggestion or intention that, if the nightmare is re-experienced, they will turn and confront their attacker. However, if the dreamer has confronted the attacker in their imagination, it is fairly likely that they will not experience this nightmare again.

Some dreamers we have worked with have been unhappy with the notion of killing their dream adversaries when confronting them. One point to note here is that often, when one turns around and confronts a dream enemy, the enemy ceases to be the aggressor and can be talked to, using a dream dialogue approach such as Gestalt. It is also worth pointing out that the Senoi's spiritual beliefs, like many other non-Western religions, saw a dream death as implying a re-birth and thus being a creative rather than destructive action.

EXAMPLE

Chris reported the following recurring nightmare:

I'm driving down the motorway in my car. I become aware that someone is driving on my tail. Whatever I do I can't get away from the car and I become more and more anxious. The car is an Aston Martin 'Vantage'; it is navy blue with cream upholstery, a cream leather hood and silver alloy wheels. The car is being driven by a middle-aged man with a 'five o'clock shadow'. I don't know who he is, although he is familiar. He is wearing polished brogues and a Crombie jacket, like my father wears.

Chris said that she had the nightmare several times and, although she had tried slowing down, speeding up, and swerving over, nothing worked. She always found herself driving faster than she wanted, and being pursued down the motorway until she felt really frightened.

In the therapy session Robyn took Chris through the nightmare, following the Senoi steps in a form of guided fantasy.

Chris decided to see if she could incorporate the fantasy into her nightmare.

(Continued)

(Continued)

During the next session she reported the following dream:

> The man was driving too close as usual, then he actually came too close and hit my car. I suddenly got angry and stopped dead and jumped out of my car to confront him.

> I said to him: 'I'm fed up with being chased all the time. You make me go faster and faster, and now you've hit my car!'

> He said to me: 'What's the problem? You're exaggerating as usual.'

> I got so angry I hit him over the head. He became like a sort of balloon man and I kept hitting him until his head somehow went right into his body. I kept hitting him and he got smaller and smaller. When he was very little I told him to go away. He had been arguing back, but as he got smaller his arguments got weaker and weaker.

> I said to him: 'Look what you've done to my car!'

> He said: 'It's only a Golf.'

> As his arguments got weaker he grew less aggressive. He said I could have his car. Then he gave me the keys and sort of flew off like a balloon. I got into his car, smelled the beautiful leather seats, turned the ignition on and heard the quiet purr of the engine. I put the car into gear and drove off, thinking to myself that I could go what speed I liked now.

In the therapy session Chris said that she had been thinking about the meaning of the nightmare. She had been feeling very hassled, with too many things to do and she wasn't sure how to cope with everything. She said that she thought that the message of the nightmare was to pay less attention to the ambitious, driving part of herself that wanted to push her harder. She realized that she could, if she wanted, find the time to look around in order to discover what she needed. She could be more discriminating and throw away any parental injunctions that were not appropriate to her.

There is some rich symbolism in this example. For example, the 'five o'clock shadow' could be a clue that the man represents what Jung called the 'shadow', that is, the unacknowledged part of ourselves. However, analysing the nightmare in objective terms is often not sufficient to allay the dreamer's fears or to allow them to feel sufficiently in control of the nightmare. Rehearsing confronting the nightmare enemy in guided fantasy can often give the dreamer enough support to tackle the nightmare in the sleeping state. There is also evidence in this nightmare of a 'topdog/underdog' conflict, which could have been worked through using Gestalt techniques, which is illustrated later in the chapter.

Gestalt approaches to nightmares

The steps to be followed in using the Gestalt approach with nightmares are essentially the same as those outlined in the previous chapter, so they will not be repeated here, although some examples of using Gestalt with nightmares will be described.

Most nightmares are primarily about internal conflicts and splits within ourselves. Thus in working with nightmares we are mostly working at Faraday's third level of interpretation, and, like her, have found Gestalt methods helpful. As described in Chapter 2, Perls thought that all dream objects or characters are split-off portions of the self that need re-integrating into the personality. Nightmares, according to Faraday, and us, are an extreme form of this split. Therefore we attempt to push away our worst fears and feelings and they come back in our dreams, in the form of nightmare creatures or objects, to haunt us. Perls believed that very negative or frightening dream objects reflect the way we have projected our own qualities outside ourselves and so experience them as alien, destructive forces beyond our control; in this way our own power turns against us.

EXAMPLE

An example of working with this kind of nightmare is Sue's recurring dream. Following the steps given in Chapter 5, Sue described her nightmare in the first person, present tense:

> The dream is always the same. In the dream I am lying in bed drifting off to sleep and I can see an enormous spider, like a scorpion. It is coming down a string towards my face. I am watching it and am powerless to move. It is getting very close to my face. I wake up screaming.

Sue reported that she had had this dream since childhood. Even now, at the age of 43, she was quite shaky with repeating the dream in the first person, present tense. Delia asked Sue what she was most curious about. Sue answered, unsurprisingly, the spider. Delia suggested that Sue should place the spider on an empty chair and talk to the spider from her own chair. Sue could only manage to address the spider if the chair was placed some way away from her. She also needed to imagine the spider safely inside a box with a lid on.

> Sue: What are you doing in my dream? Why are you frightening me? Who are you?

(Continued)

(Continued)

Delia suggested that Sue should become the spider and answer. Sue was very frightened, but Delia held her hand as she moved to the other chair.

> Spider: I'm squashed up here in this box and am pressed down by this lid and can hardly breathe. I'm going to push the lid off.

As Sue pushed the lid off, her mood changed instantly from abject fear to almost spitting anger.

> Spider: I'm absolutely sick and tired of being put down by you. You are always so clever and pretty and everybody notices you. Just who the hell do you think you are?

Delia asked Sue who she was shouting at. Sue replied that she was shouting at her twin sister, Ann. Delia suggested that Sue put Ann in the empty chair and express her resentments using a form of words 'I resent you for . . .', repeating this for as long as necessary. After about five minutes Sue had expressed her resentments to Ann and her anger had somewhat abated. (It is important at this stage for the therapist to encourage the dreamer to express as many of her resentments as she is able to, since this allows the completion of the unfinished emotional business.) Delia then asked Sue to move across and be Ann.

> Ann: I never knew that you felt like this. I couldn't help being bigger. I always got into trouble if I didn't look after you. Things were always my fault. Now I know why we've not been very close.

At this point Sue moved back into her own chair. She looked very tired and sad and Delia asked her to express this. Sue chose to stop the dialogue at this point. (Even if the therapist thinks that more can be done, the wishes of the dreamer to continue or stop working should always be respected.)

Sue then shared how she had been the smaller and weaker of twins. She had resented her sister as a child but had been scared to express this. In adult life the twins were not very close.

Although Sue would like to have been closer, something always got in the way and she found herself being irritated by her sister, feeling guilty for this and avoiding her.

This nightmare is a very dramatic example of how Sue had become alienated from her angry feelings towards her twin sister. She had projected these feelings onto the nightmare creature of the spider, who had then come back in this recurring dream throughout her life to haunt her. After Sue was able to confront the spider her nightmare stopped completely and never returned. Sue reported later that she had tentatively begun to communicate better with her twin sister and felt more hopeful about their relationship.

Although non-threatening recurring dreams do occur, it is often the case that recurring dreams may occur when similar frightening feelings that were present in the child re-occur in the adult, particularly when the feelings are very intense. These dreams are often about internal splits, and a Gestalt approach is the method of choice with recurring, but non post-traumatic nightmares. It is possible that with recurring dreams the message keeps being repeated until we pay attention to it.

Perls's concept of the 'topdog' and the 'underdog' was mentioned earlier and it was described how the self-righteous, dominant topdog can be locked into a battle with the overwhelmed, wheedling underdog. This is a very relevant concept when we are dealing with nightmares. Often the two are locked into a battle, pulling in opposite directions and causing the paralysis often felt in nightmares. Ann Faraday called these 'the hounds of hell' to reflect the torment often felt. Faraday says that the topdog sometimes appears as the 'enemy figure' in nightmares with themes of attack, violence and intrusion. In this case it is important to make the power of the topdog subservient. Faraday considers that the underdog often appears as a shadowy figure or as an earthy symbol and may represent basic or child needs. It is critical to allow the underdog element the possibility to express itself powerfully in the dialogue because it is important for the dreamer to recognize and own these unmet emotional needs. It is part of the process of working with the nightmare for the dreamer to be able to reduce the power of the topdog, whereas the underdog needs to be supported. This is because in waking life we are often out of balance with the topdog part of ourselves, preventing the expression of more emotional and creative needs. The judgemental, moralistic topdog is similar to Eric Berne's (1964) concept of the critical parent: the part of ourselves created by injunctions we have swallowed from our parents exhorting us to be good, perfect, work hard and so on. Our lives may be ruled by these voices and they may not be appropriate to our present life. The whining, masochistic underdog is similar to Eric Berne's concept of the adapted child. This is the part of oneself that has adapted by attempting to live up to the demands of the topdog but complains and attempts to sabotage the demands of the topdog and never gets their real emotional needs met. The nightmare can be an expression of these conflicts and the job of the therapist is to help the dreamer to achieve balance and integration between the parts of the personality. The next nightmare example illustrates a typical topdog/underdog conflict.

EXAMPLE

Lauren reported the following nightmare in the first person, present tense:

> I am lying in bed. I am on my own and it is very dark. I can hear creaking, as if someone is moving around outside the room. Slowly, almost imperceptibly at first, I can see the door to my bedroom opening. I hold my breath and go

(Continued)

(Continued)

completely cold with terror. My bed is behind the door and I see a man's hand, with a knife in it, appear slowly round the door. Everything seems to be going very slowly and I am completely paralysed. The knife is raised ready to strike. Then I wake up in a cold sweat.

After speaking as the different elements of the dream, Lauren was invited to carry out a conversation between the knife and herself in bed. Here is a summary of the dialogue:

> *Knife:* I'm coming for you. Get up! You've got to do what I say.
>
> *Lauren:* Go away. You're frightening me. Leave me alone, I haven't done you any harm . . .
>
> *Knife:* You're weak. I'm going to kill you because I despise you.
>
> *Lauren:* I'm fed up with being ruled by you. I'm sick of obeying your orders. Nothing I do is good enough for you. You're always ordering me around. I can never seem to please you.
>
> *Knife:* I despise you because you're always dithering around. Why can't you be more decisive? You should get on with your life.
>
> *Lauren:* You won't survive long if you don't let me slow down a bit. This pressure is too much for both of us.
>
> *Knife:* Maybe I am overdoing things a bit. I'll try to slow down – but don't go too slow or I'll have to shake you up again.
>
> *Lauren:* If you don't put so much pressure on me and set a more reasonable pace, I'll try to keep up.

As this topdog/underdog conflict emerged, Lauren began to recognize that it reminded her of how she had felt as a child, when she had been criticized and nagged by her mother. At the time of the nightmare Lauren was feeling rather pressured at work by her new, dynamic manager. She realized that the knife/topdog represented the perfectionist, critical part of herself that was often in conflict with the Lauren in bed, the underdog part of herself that didn't want to be continually striving. She chose to continue the dialogue, and after a time it took the following shape:

> *Knife:* I only want what's best for you. I want you to get on.
>
> *Lauren:* I want what's best for me too. I want you to recognize that you don't always know best for both of us.
>
> *Knife:* Well what do you want then? You won't do very well without me.

Lauren: You're right, I suppose I couldn't do without you. But I'm sick of being threatened by you. I don't want you to go away altogether, but I don't want you to threaten me either. I'm not going to let myself be pressurized by you. I want to enjoy life a bit.

Knife: Let me know if I put too much pressure on you again.

Lauren: I certainly will.

Lauren gave a big sigh and smiled at this point. She said she felt satisfied. She went on to explain that this dialogue was making her think about her work situation. There had recently been a reshuffle at work and she had felt that she wasn't doing well enough. She now realized that in fact she had been putting a lot of pressure on herself, which had come from inside herself rather than from the new manager, who had actually been quite helpful and friendly.

Perhaps the most important feature common to the methods for working with nightmares is best summed up by Ann Faraday, who considers that 'a willingness to confront and embrace the things you fear in yourself is the essential clue to integration' (1974: 261). This statement is clearly illustrated by a participant in a recent workshop who reported a nightmare by saying: 'I had a dream in which I was being chased down a corridor. I did not know what was chasing me but there were these awful banshee noises. Eventually I turned round and I was amazed to see that it was me chasing myself. It was actually me making all those noises.'

The next section of the chapter considers the utility of lucid dreaming. If the dreamer is able to become lucid in the dream, that is, to become aware that they are dreaming, then they are able to manipulate the dream or nightmare by changing the storyline or ending, confronting the enemy, by introducing a dream helper or by other methods. All of this can be done without the dreamer actually waking up.

Lucid dreaming

The characteristic of lucid dreams is for the dreamer to know that they are asleep and dreaming. Thus in lucid dreams we are able to consciously observe and control our dream content. Writers on this subject think that it is possible for most of us to attain some degree of lucidity in our dreams, and that the experience of lucid dreaming is, to some extent, a learned skill. Often the first awareness of lucidity for many of us is towards the end of a nightmare when we become aware that we are dreaming and wake ourselves up. One way of increasing the period of lucidity is to move forwards from this point saying to oneself, 'I know this is only a dream, I will remain asleep a bit longer' or 'I know I am dreaming and therefore I can't actually be harmed.' A key element of lucid dreaming is, therefore, that the dreamer knows that the dream can be controlled, at least to some extent, and can mostly decide what to do in the dream. However, although the dreamer is conscious and can take decisions, the dream still follows dream logic and contains the bizarre characteristics of dreams. In fact, the dreamer is aware that they are dreaming and not awake because they notice the strange irrational events that only happen in dreams. La Berge has written extensively on this subject in his books on *Lucid Dreaming* (1985, 2004), and suggests techniques that will help to induce lucid dreams. The author's experience is that people vary considerably in the extent to which they are able to induce lucid dreaming. For most people the experience is momentary and can affect critical points in the dream, which otherwise continues as normal. My friend Robyn is able to fly to order in her dreams. Thus, if she finds herself in a sticky situation, she becomes lucid and says to herself 'This is a dream and I can fly in my dreams; I will fly out of this situation.'

Tips for the therapist working with lucid dreams

1 Two necessary ingredients for lucid dreaming are good motivation and good dream recall, so it is important to have a dream diary and to practise and develop these skills first.
2 La Berge suggests that the dreamer needs to practise carrying their daytime alertness into sleep; this is so that they can recognize the peculiar characteristics of their dreams and thus become aware that they are dreaming. It is suggested that reality testing is an important part of generating lucid dreaming. The dreamers need to ask themselves how they know whether they are dreaming or not. For example, in Robyn's experience of flying she is able to realize that she is in a dream by the fact that she is flying. Essentially, the point is for the dreamers to recognize whether they are awake or dreaming.
3 La Berge suggests that the dreamer question their state of consciousness during the waking state, actually asking themselves whether they are dreaming at several points during the day, in order to develop a critically reflective attitude towards their state of consciousness.
4 The dreamer should incubate the intention to dream lucidly prior to going to sleep.
5 La Berge developed a technique whereby he counted '... one ... I am dreaming ... two ... I am dreaming ... three ... I am dreaming' and so on. He suggests that by the time the dreamer reaches a count of 40, hopefully they will be dreaming.

Following these steps does not guarantee success and people vary in their ability. Where dreamers already have some degree of lucidity, they develop their skills and work creatively with their nightmares in the dreaming state as the following examples show. However, those dreamers who are rarely lucid prefer to use the methods outlined earlier in the chapter. It is not recommended that people who have had any kind of psychotic episode or who exhibit borderline characteristics attempt to induce lucid dreaming. Therapists who want to read more about lucid dreaming can refer to La Berge (1985, 2004).

EXAMPLES

The following two nightmares are from Annette, who was a skilled lucid dreamer but who was not aware of how lucid dreaming could help her to feel more in control in her nightmares. In the first nightmare Annette uses 'face and conquer' methods to confront a dream enemy. In a later nightmare she calls on the previous dream enemy, who is now a 'dream friend', to help her. Annette described her dreams in the first person:

> In this nightmare I am walking down a corridor, and I know that I have to get to the other end. Somehow it feels like a matter of life and death that I get down the corridor. Suddenly, I see that there are two snarling Doberman Pinscher dogs barring my way. At this point I become lucid and work out that if I grab the dogs' muzzles, I can get past them. I am still rather frightened but I manage to grab their muzzles and get past the dogs. Then I walk into the next room and sit down on a large comfortable settee to have a rest. Suddenly one of the Doberman dogs comes around the open door, walks up to me and smiles. He nudges at me with his nose and then, to my surprise, jumps up and sits on my knee. He says, 'My name is Bruno and I will be your friend.' That is the end of the dream.

Annette became lucid in this dream at the point where she was frightened and needed to find a way to confront her enemy. Her lucidity allowed her to overcome her fear sufficiently to find a useful strategy. This dream is a good example of how, when confronted, a dream enemy can become a dream friend. This can be of lasting benefit, as can be seen by the next example:

> I am walking in the country when I see a large, attractive country house. Although there is no 'For Sale' sign, I decide that I want to buy the house. I knock at the front door; a man answers and I ask if I can see round the house. The man tells me that, if I wait in the conservatory, someone will come and take me round soon. As I walk round the house to the conservatory, I look in the windows and see that all the rooms are full of shit. I sit in the conservatory and have a cup of tea. Presently, a young woman fetches me to show me round the house. When we go in, however, there is no sign of the shit. The house is beautiful, with polished wood floors. We walk round and then go upstairs. I go into a room. It's dark and as I enter I see that the floor is sloping away from me towards the window. The floor then seems to

(Continued)

(Continued)

slope more steeply and I fall and begin sliding down towards the window wall. As I slide I see that a gap has opened up between the floor and the window wall. I see all the other floors beneath me and think that I am going to fall. I have my feet wedged on the window wall and I am grasping the floor with my fingers. The gap is widening and I realize that I am going to fall and die. At this point I become lucid and call for Bruno to help me. There is a flash of white light and a great Doberman comes flying through the air. He grabs me by my collar and we fly out through the window. As we fly, I see beautiful countryside far below. Bruno asks me if I am all right. We see a beautiful apple orchard and start to descend. We land and Bruno sets me gently down. As he does so I say, 'I didn't want a big, rambling house anyway.' As I say the words there is a large crack, like a clap of thunder. I look round and see that the large house has turned into a narrow terraced house and know that was what I wanted.

This dream is a particularly lovely example of calling for help in the form of a dream friend. Bruno regularly appears in Annette's dreams and she can call on him when she needs to by becoming lucid. It is also possible to call on a dream friend by using the dream incubation or guided re-entry methods. Annette did spend some time considering the meaning of this dream, which made most sense to her when working at the third level of interpretation.

Generally, the same broad principles for working with adults' nightmares also apply to working with children. The next section outlines some general principles when working with children's nightmares.

Children's nightmares

Irrespective of the kind of nightmare the child has had, therapists should work towards empowering children to become active, rather than passive, both in their lives and in their dreams. For children, the boundaries between reality and imagination, or waking and dreaming, are far less fixed than for adults. Therefore it is relatively easy for suggestions given by the therapist to the child in waking life to be carried by the child into their dream. This capacity means that many children can, relatively effortlessly, change their nightmares so that they are more active and in control.

Before attempting to work on the actual nightmare content, it is essential for therapists to assess what might be causing the nightmares. Although nightmares are especially frequent in young children and seem to be related to basic childhood fears, such as loss of people close to the child, or fears of the child's own aggressive impulses, it is important for the therapist also to look for environmental situations or family dynamics that may make the child feel especially helpless or vulnerable. In older children, nightmares increase during periods of stress and especially in conditions involving helplessness. It was mentioned earlier in the chapter that presence of nightmares in children can be a primary indicator of sexual and physical abuse. In cases where identifiable causes can be found, treatment should not be aimed initially specifically at the nightmare, but should be directed at providing structured support for the child in waking life. However, empowering the child to deal with the nightmare actively can complement attempts to make the child feel less vulnerable in waking life.

General principles for the therapist to follow when working with children's nightmares

1 The therapist should teach the child to confront and conquer danger in dreams, and to fight rather than to run and hide, but also to befriend rather than to brutalize. Suggestions can be made by the therapist, either directly to the child or indirectly through the parents. The child can usually incorporate into their nightmare direct suggestions made in waking life.
   Geraldine chose to take a piece of soft velvet to bed with her. When the monster came in her nightmare, Geraldine was able to imagine that she had an enormous cloak that had magic powers of dissolving anything that it was thrown over. In her nightmare Geraldine was able to turn round and throw her cloak over the monster chasing her. Josh was able to take a toy sword to bed with him. He was able to imagine, in his nightmares, that this became 'Excalibur', the sword with which he was able to fight and conquer the dragon in his nightmare. Once the general principle has been suggested to the child, he can usually find his own ingenious adaptation of it. For example, Delia's son, Ben, was able to turn himself into a 'transformer', a children's robot toy, before he went to sleep. Thus Ben felt that he would be protected in his dreams by being able to 'transform' himself if he needed.
2 The therapist should teach the child to call on dream friends for help when needed. It is important to convey the concept that the child can do something about the terrifying situation. For example, four-year-old Lisa was able to imagine that the teddy that she normally took to bed with her would come alive if she called to him in her nightmare, and would come to her aid. Obviously the type of dream friend will vary according to the age and sophistication of the child.
3 The therapist can suggest that children are given stories with which they can identify that will provide a model for successful confrontation.
4 The therapist can suggest that children are taught appropriate skills in waking life that can help them cope with dream disasters. After Sam had seen an item

(Continued)

(Continued)

on the television news concerning a family who had died when their house had burnt down, he had nightmares of fires. In waking life Sam was taken to the local fire station and shown around. He was also taught how to dial the emergency services on the telephone. After this his nightmares quickly faded.

5 The therapist can encourage the child to explore and enjoy his pleasant dreams and can also show him how he can incorporate them into his waking life. This might be by writing stories, drawing pictures, or by making other creative use of the dream material. Working with dreams can help to remove the fear from them. We think it is important for the therapist to encourage a child to express bad dreams in some waking form, either by talking or by artistic product.

6 With smaller children the therapist can encourage the child to take favourite toys, books or music to bed with them. It can be enormously reassuring and consoling for small children to hold their favourite stuffed animal or doll. Patricia Garfield (1984) introduces the concept of the 'dreamworthy bed'. This involves helping the child to make her bed a special and enjoyable place to be in. It is not generally helpful for parents to send the child to her bed as a punishment, since this links bed with unpleasant associations.

7 The therapist can encourage parents to provide toys that suggest the nightmare content. This can give the child an opportunity to act out fantasies. Playing out nightmares can help a child practise more satisfactory conclusions. For example, Neil was able to act out his fantasy of conquering his nightmare enemy in play using his 'anti-monster' rocket launcher and gun.

Of course, it is a good idea for the therapist to look for long-term solutions and removal of the nightmare source, wherever possible. However, this is not always realistically possible, and the strategies suggested above can help children cope by increasing their feelings of control both in their dreaming as well as in their waking life.

Confronting the dream enemy

As suggested above, it is helpful to encourage children to draw their dreams and nightmares or to make another creative product from their nightmare. A creative intervention for children and adults alike involves drawing their scary dream. The following exercise is adapted from Ann Sayre Wiseman (1986) and is called 'confronting the dream enemy'. This can be seen as a form of 'face and conquer' intervention. Like re-writing the nightmare, this can be done by the adult client alone at home. However, in the case of children, it is much more supportive for the therapist and/or parent to work through the following exercise with the child.

Steps for 'confronting the dream enemy'

1 Recall a nightmare.
2 Draw the nightmare scene with yourself in the picture. As you are drawing, focus on your feelings. The helper may need to encourage the dreamer to vocalize these.
3 Draw into the picture ways of feeling safe.
   - Think how you can help the dream ego (dreamer).
   - Think how you can control the dream enemy so that you can talk to it.
   - Examples:
     - Protect yourself from the enemy by drawing a cage around it.
     - Put a barrier between yourself and the enemy.
     - Hide from the enemy.
     - Bring in help from dream friends.
4 From a safe place, establish communication with the enemy.
   - Examples:
     - By conversation, by telephone, by email, by text.
       Ask the enemy what it wants. Establish a dialogue with the enemy.
     - What would you like to tell the enemy?
     - What is its point of view?
     - If there was a fair solution, what would it be?
     - See yourself finding a solution.
5 Draw another picture to show how the nightmare is resolved.
6 Make a new statement to summarise what the dream ego is doing/feeling.

I have used this exercise with adults and children as well as with people with a learning disability. It can be a helpful intervention for anyone who finds it difficult, for whatever reason, to verbalize their feelings.

EXAMPLE

Delia and a colleague ran a dream workshop in a centre for adults with moderate learning disabilities. The workers told us that the residents often suffered from nightmares but had very few resources to manage these. Each resident was paired with a helper for doing the exercise. Delia worked with Tom, who experienced longstanding difficulties with nightmares and had a recurring nightmare of a burglar breaking into his house and attacking him. Delia helped Tom to work through the steps above. At stage 3 Tom drew into his picture an enormous policeman's helmet. He thought that a policeman would protect him from harm. Tom was not really able

(Continued)

(Continued)

enough to complete stages 4, 5 and 6 but he appeared delighted with the picture he had drawn and enthusiastically coloured in his large policeman's helmet. Delia heard from staff that Tom appeared much happier to go to sleep and that this action appeared to have resolved his nightmare. This is an illustration of the power of both empowerment and finding one's own solution. For Tom, and for many other people, especially children, it is the drawing of their own solution and not the dialogue that brings about the resolution.

The methods that have been outlined are not mutually exclusive and can be mixed and used creatively together. In all cases sympathetic listening, discussion and some measure of encouragement should accompany the dreamwork. It is important that the helper reflects the real feelings of anxiety or terror, and the accompanying helplessness, that the nightmare engenders, without trying to minimize these. However, the critical aspect is to encourage and empower dreamers, whether they are adults or children, to find ways to overcome these through their own resources.

Summary

Nightmares are frightening dreams from REM sleep that normally awaken the dreamer. Two broad approaches, namely 'storyline alteration' and 'face and conquer', are outlined. Interventions for each of these approaches, including the use of 'lucid dreaming', are described. Some examples of using the Gestalt approach to working with nightmares are also included. The same broad principles, but adapted for children, are presented. These are followed by a drawing method entitled 'confronting the dream enemy', which is especially created for children but which can also be utilized for adults as well as for people with a learning disability.

7

Post-traumatic Nightmares and Night Terrors

This chapter covers two areas where sleep and dream disturbances are presented as a major symptom for which people are seeking treatment. The difficulties described here range in severity from the major psychological problem of post-traumatic stress disorder (PTSD) and working with survivors of abuse to a lesser parental worry about a child's night terrors.

Trauma

The current *Diagnostic and Statistical Manual of Mental Disorders* (DSMIV) classes an experience as a traumatic event when '(1) The person experienced, witnessed or was confronted with an event or events that involved actual or threatened death or serious injury, or a threat to the physical integrity of self or others; (2) the persons response involved intense fear, helplessness, or horror' (APA, 2004: 467). Examples of traumatic events are serious accidents, military combat, violent personal physical or sexual assault, and natural or man-made disasters. 'Complex PTSD' is the name sometimes given, although not an official diagnosis, to people who have repeatedly experienced severe neglect as an adult or child, or who have suffered severe repeated violence as an adult, such as torture or abusive imprisonment.

There are three main clusters of symptoms. The first, often called 're-living', involves day-time flashbacks and nightmares. These can be very realistic and intense and, as well as imagery of the event, the person may feel the emotions and physical sensations of what happened. The second cluster of symptoms is avoidance and numbing, whereby people attempt to distance themselves by distraction and avoidance of people and places that remind them of the event as well as trying not to talk about it. They may also deal with the emotional pain by trying to become emotionally numb and possibly less communicative. The third cluster involves being 'on guard', and people stay alert at all times and find it difficult to relax. This 'hypervigilance' also makes people anxious, jumpy and irritable, and people find it hard to sleep. There can also be other symptoms such as muscle- and headaches, or substance abuse (Royal College of Psychiatrists, 2010).

Nearly everyone will have symptoms of post-traumatic stress for the first month or so after a traumatic event, and symptoms that arise within the first month may come under the category of acute stress disorder (ASD). Many people slowly come to terms with what has happened and their stress reactions start to disappear, but about one in three find that their symptoms carry on, as though the process has got stuck. The symptoms of post-traumatic stress, though normal in themselves, become PTSD when they go on for too long.

Post-traumatic nightmares

Although most of us have experienced the occasional nightmare, for trauma survivors nightmares are much more common (Duke, Allen, Rozee & Bommaritto, 2007), and for trauma survivors who go on to develop PTSD the incidence of those reporting nightmares can vary from 52 per cent to 96 per cent (Neylan et al., 1998; Davis, Byrd, Rhudy & Wright, 2007). Post-traumatic nightmares have an obvious precipitating event, although not all nightmares that occur following trauma are a direct replay of the trauma. Research suggests that about half of those experiencing them may have post-traumatic nightmares that exactly replicate the traumatic event. People diagnosed with PTSD are more likely to have nightmares that are exact replays than are trauma survivors without PTSD (Davis et al., 2007).

Studies suggest that post-traumatic nightmares have somewhat different physical characteristics from ordinary nightmares. Some workers consider post-traumatic nightmares to be more like night terrors (which will be described later in the chapter), since the sufferer often awakes in terror, early in the night, with a scream, autonomic arousal, and occasionally a sleep-walking episode. Thus some researchers have suggested that a traumatic nightmare may be a phenomenon of arousal rather than a true nightmare. In fact, traumatic nightmares can apparently arise out of REM sleep as well as sleep stage 2, and this makes them somewhat different from nightmares or night terrors (Germain & Nielson, 2003). In other ways, traumatic nightmares do resemble ordinary nightmares in that they are usually experienced as dreams; also, many are resolved and disappear fairly quickly by merging with other dream content and becoming more a part of ordinary dream life.

Acute post-traumatic nightmares

Acute post-traumatic nightmares are fairly common in children, where they probably occur after most serious traumatic events. However, since they are usually resolved within a few weeks, and children rarely develop the post-traumatic stress syndrome seen in adults, children with post-traumatic nightmares are not often brought for therapy. If a therapist's help is sought, it is most helpful to encourage the child to talk about their experiences as much as possible, and to enable them to connect up the experience to the rest of their life.

Acute post-traumatic nightmares are also common in adults who have been involved in severe traumas, such as horrific road accidents. These can be intensified if the individual is feeling particularly vulnerable at the time of the trauma. In most of these cases the nightmares will fade fairly rapidly, although therapy can be helpful as it can accelerate the process. The main goal in treatment is to assist the individual to integrate the event into their waking life. This can best be achieved by giving the person a chance to talk about the traumatic event and to re-live it in waking life in the therapy sessions.

EXAMPLE

Martin came for therapy when he was having difficulty in dealing with a particularly horrific road accident in which he had been involved. He had been in a multiple-car pile-up and was the first on the scene to discover that, in the most badly damaged car, the woman driver had gone through the windscreen and been decapitated. She had been eight months pregnant at the time and doctors were unable to save the baby. The image of the roadside scene haunted Martin, both in post-traumatic nightmares and in waking flashbacks. He felt unable to talk about his feelings or describe the scene to those closest to him, since most people were very shocked at hearing his story. Martin found that he needed to protect people from the horrific event that he had witnessed, and therefore had been unable to work through his own feelings. At the time of the accident Martin was 21 and had a strong vocation to enter the priesthood. In fact, he had been about to enter a seminary. Martin's faith was considerably shaken by the tragedy and so he felt that the very foundation of his being, not to mention his future career, had been turned upside-down.

During therapy Delia encouraged Martin to re-tell the nightmare and the traumatic event in a number of ways. He was asked, many times, to recall and re-live the emotions associated with the trauma. It was important to try to understand, as far as possible, what were the worst aspects of the trauma for him, and to try to provide understanding and support, as well as an opportunity for Martin to

(Continued)

(Continued)

re-experience the emotions. Delia encouraged Martin to attempt to connect up the experience with his ordinary life in the safe setting that therapy provided. It was also important to discuss his hopeless feelings that things would never get any better. It can be important that therapy for post-traumatic nightmares is initiated quickly, so that the nightmares do not become chronic and therefore more difficult to treat. However, the counselling or therapy need not be long-term; with appropriate help, recovery can be rapid. After three months of weekly sessions, Martin had largely recovered. The nightmares, flashbacks and intrusive thoughts had vanished. Martin had been able to reconcile the tragedy sufficiently to recover his faith and to go to church again. He had also obtained a place at college to train to be a teacher and was looking forward to his future again. Of course, the memory of the tragedy will always remain with Martin, but he had been able to integrate it sufficiently so that he could live comfortably, without it haunting his life.

Chronic post-traumatic nightmares

While most post-trauma nightmares dissipate fairly quickly within weeks of the traumatic event, as in Martin's case, the post-traumatic nightmares can become chronic and persist for many years. Hartmann (1984) commented that these are not typical REM nightmares; they can also occur when the individual is going to sleep, and daytime reminders can set off waking flashbacks.

Davis (2009) has suggested a three-factor model of post-traumatic nightmare development and maintenance involving predisposing, precipitating and perpetuating factors in understanding chronic post-traumatic nightmares. Predisposing factors might include pre-trauma psychological disorders, personality traits and lifestyle characteristics that may increase the person's vulnerability to developing nightmares. The relationship between chronic nightmares and personality traits and psychopathology remains unclear. However, there has been support for Hartmann's (1984) idea of 'thin boundaries', which consists of open-mindedness, sensitivity, vulnerability, creativity and artistic ability, being associated with frequent nightmares. Another possible vulnerability factor might be high arousability and anxiety which has been associated with sleep and nightmare problems post-trauma. A pre-existing avoidant coping style has also been postulated to play a role in nightmare maintenance following trauma, though this has not been evidenced (Davis, 2009).

The main precipitating factor for post-traumatic nightmares is obviously the trauma itself, and certain aspects of the trauma may be particularly important for increased risk of nightmares. For example, being the victim of aggression can increase the risk of experiencing nightmares (Ohayon &

Shapiro, 2000). Much of the early research on post-traumatic nightmares was carried out with Vietnam veterans. For example, Hartmann showed that those who developed chronic post-traumatic nightmares in combat were unusually young, around age 18. He suggested that the nightmare sufferers 'may have been in a particularly vulnerable state – they had formed very intense bonds of a narcissistic type with one or several buddies in their unit' (1984: 242). It was when one of their close friends was killed that the young soldiers felt particularly damaged or betrayed and started to experience the nightmares. Additionally, survivors may feel that they, and not their friends, should have died. This is the phenomenon known as 'survivor guilt'. Hartmann also suggested that sometimes the nightmares can be triggered later, if the person suffers an additional loss, for example of a girlfriend. Thus he concludes: 'these serious nightmares occurred only when there was an unusually severe psychological wound. They also occurred in young men who had a part of themselves torn out, usually by the death of a close buddy' (p. 242). Hartmann went on to suggest that in severe cases, where the individual is not, for whatever reason, able to integrate the experience into their life, it somehow becomes split off, isolated and 'encapsulated'. This separate memory can sometimes be sparked-off by a variety of shifts in brain physiology, usually in sleep, but also in waking life. Once the 'walling-up', as Hartmann described it, has occurred, and the nightmares have become chronic, treatment is much more difficult. Therefore, Hartmann suggests that treatment should be carried out early enough after the traumatic event to prevent the splitting-off of the traumatic material.

As suggested by Krakow and Zadra (2006), what initiates nightmares may not be what maintains them. The initial nightmares can continue to evolve through other factors becoming a learned condition and vicious cycle that maintains the problem over time. Davis (2009) suggests how this can happen: people mostly awake from terrifying nightmares in a state of high arousal and associated physiological responses such as sweating which, together with the nightmare content, can serve as trauma cues to further heighten arousal. Nightmares also create significant sleep disruption and disturbance. The sleep deprivation and its effects of lack of concentration and emotional lability, together with thoughts of the nightmare, can lead to increased daytime distress and arousal which the person may try to manage by avoidance-coping strategies. Avoiding thinking about the nightmare means that it cannot be processed and understood and thus is unlikely to be assimilated and integrated. In this way the nightmare is likely to be maintained and the person may experience anticipatory anxiety at the thought of night-time and sleep. This may be exacerbated by distorted cognitions and negative self-talk such as 'I'm never going to be able to sleep without nightmares again'. Some people try to reduce anxiety by substance use, notably alcohol and pills, while others may attempt to avoid sleep until they become extremely exhausted. Davis likens these tactics to safety behaviours, which are designed to reduce the likelihood of a nightmare through restricting sleep. Often these behaviours may work initially, but will not work in the longer term. A good example is the use of alcohol, which may initially help people to fall asleep more quickly but will disrupt sleep and cause a REM rebound, which itself is likely to produce nightmares later in the night. A slightly adapted form of Davis's (2009) 'vicious cycle' model is shown in Figure 7.1.

Figure 7.1   Three-factor model of nightmare development and maintenance (from *Treating Post-Trauma Nightmares, A Cognitive Behavioral Approach*, Davis, 2009. Reproduced with the permission of Springer Publishing Company, LLC)

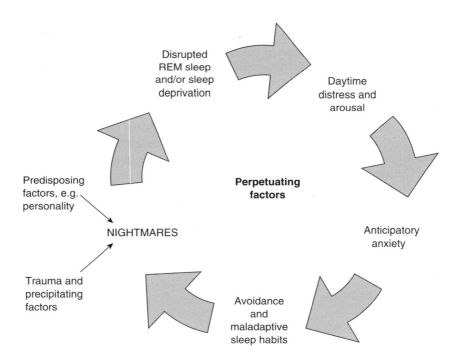

EXAMPLE

Harry was 60 when he was referred as suffering from chronic anxiety. His main symptoms were chronic post-traumatic nightmares of severe intensity about four or five times a week. As a result of these, Harry had become increasingly anxious and was fearful about going out on busy public transport or into crowded places.

He was also frightened of loud, particularly shrill noises. Harry was scared to go to bed and often sat up all night. He slept on his own, since his night-time screams, his intense agitation and movement in bed and his profuse sweating disturbed his wife, who was in extremely poor health. Harry had felt increasingly unable to cope, hence his self-confidence was very low. Harry's experience in the Korean War, 30 years earlier, had included his two best friends being killed, being the only survivor of his company during one attack, and being severely wounded on another occasion. Subsequently, Harry suffered from post-traumatic night-mares, re-living these and other experiences for about seven or eight years after the events. It was clear that Harry had felt not only intense fear and loss but also 'survivor guilt'. After coronary by-pass surgery five years earlier, Harry's feelings of intense fear and helplessness returned. The experience triggered the return of the post-traumatic nightmares.

During therapy Harry talked about his early life. When he was four he had broken his leg badly and had spent two or three months in hospital. His mother was only able to visit once and Harry remembered sobbing for her. Harry's family disintegrated when he was about six and his brothers were sent to Australia. Harry had only vague memories of his father, although he remembered rows and beatings. When he was seven he was put into an orphanage with his two sisters, who were later adopted and sent to Wales. He was intensely unhappy in the orphanage and remembered being bullied but learning to control his feelings. During the time he was in the orphanage Harry had only been sent six letters from his mother, who died when he was 14. He had once had contact with an older brother by accident, but the brother had died 15 years before Harry came to therapy. Harry had initially worked on a farm but had then joined the army. The times in the army, before the Korean War, were among some of the happiest Harry had known because of the friends he had made and the spirit of comrade-ship. Harry had been discharged from the army with 40 per cent disability from gunshot wounds but had enjoyed his later working life as a foreman, although he had always been prone to feeling stressed. He had been forced to retire because of heart problems and had four heart attacks followed by surgery. Harry described himself as somewhat of a loner, although he had married and had two children, who had now married and left home.

Harry found therapy difficult, since he was ashamed of his feelings, regarded them as a weakness, and had not discussed his experiences in detail with anyone before. Therapy entailed giving Harry permission to describe the events during the Korean War and enabling him to discuss and acknowledge his feelings. Delia taught Harry about post-traumatic stress syndrome and survivor guilt and this ena-bled him to put his feelings into a context. In particular, Harry learnt about post-traumatic nightmares and how they could relate to his waking state. Delia asked Harry to keep a diary of his nightmares. So Harry recorded the date and time of waking. He briefly recorded the content of the nightmare, what he did after waking, and also rated the intensity of the nightmare distress on a scale from 1 to 5.

The data Harry recorded allowed four true post-traumatic nightmares to be identified. The first two nightmares related to Harry's experience of being in a small

(Continued)

(Continued)

scouting party that was sent ahead of the main company. They became trapped and cut off and were forced to witness, from a hillside, the entire company being shelled and decimated. In the first nightmare Harry heard and saw the shells exploding and saw his mates being blown up. He was forced to watch the dead and dying, from the hillside, through binoculars, while keeping watch. In particular one soldier was left hanging dead in a tree for a week until it was safe enough for the dead to be reached. The second nightmare involved the image of this particular soldier in the tree. Harry expressed his feelings of fear, guilt, horror and helplessness. In the third nightmare Harry was trapped, wounded, in a trench. He heard the whine of the shells falling but was unable to move and woke up screaming. The last nightmare involved Harry's experiences in hospital after he was wounded. He was lying on a trolley held down by bottles and drips. The doctor approached him to inject him in the throat. Harry was in intense pain and tried to cry out but he was unable to get the words out. He tried to move but couldn't. Again he woke up screaming. All these nightmares were exact replications of Harry's actual experiences. There was also a fifth nightmare, which was more like an ordinary recurring nightmare, in which Harry was in bed and heard someone coming into the bedroom to get him. Harry tried to lash out but was paralysed by fear and woke up screaming and thrashing about.

As therapy progressed, Delia taught Harry relaxation and provided him with a relaxation and sleep tape. Harry was able to use the tape to help him get to sleep as well as to calm him down when he woke with the nightmares. Harry also learned some strategies for coping with his feelings; in particular he learned to be able to acknowledge them to his wife as well as to his only close male friend. Delia also encouraged Harry to embark on a series of progressively more difficult outings so that he was able to travel to various places on public transport. Although Harry was always terrified of hospitals, he began to be able to accompany his wife on her frequent out-patient trips to hospital and was also able to visit an old friend when he was in hospital. As Harry began to achieve the small goals he set himself, he began to feel more confident and in control. The nightmares lessened significantly in frequency and intensity and Harry felt more in control and able to deal with the nightmares he did have. He was even able to go on two short holidays.

However, although Harry's anxiety lessened considerably, the nightmares never completely disappeared. Many events in his life re-triggered the nightmares. These included the death of his close friend, the hospitalization of his wife, a return of his angina, and the Gulf War. As well as these major events, other events such as bonfire night and hearing the whine of fireworks, hearing children screaming and even seeing war and hospital scenes on television were enough to spark off the nightmares. Harry remained very avoidant and was never able to cope with cognitive exposure or imagery-based approaches for treating his PTSD and his nightmares. Harry's case has been included, even though treatment was not overly successful, because he illustrates some of the typical features, and the case demonstrates some of the difficulties of working with chronic post-traumatic nightmares.

Treatment for post-traumatic nightmares

It is important that any treatment for nightmares is carried out within the overall context of treatment for PTSD. This will include a comprehensive assessment of the client, including a risk assessment. Treatment needs also to include psychoeducation about PTSD, nightmares and sleep. There are a number of evidence-based treatments for PTSD (Foa, Keane & Friedman, 2000), although these broad-based treatments may be less successful for sleep disturbances including nightmares (Zayfert & DeViva, 2004). Most of the evidence-based PTSD treatments involve exposure techniques; however, they generally don't include direct exposure to nightmare content (Davis, 2009). The most well-known and best-evidenced intervention is imagery rehearsal therapy, which is described below. Apart from its evidence base, which has been reviewed by Davis (2009), it is a brief and accessible intervention.

Imagery rehearsal therapy (IRT)

Imagery rehearsal therapy (IRT) was initially developed by Kellner, Neidhardt, Krakow and Pathak (1992), and has been modified and adapted by Barry Krakow (2004) mainly for groups of survivors of sexual abuse suffering from PTSD to reduce the number, intensity and intrusiveness of nightmares. The approach does not explore the meaning of the dream in depth but rather at the behavioural manifest level to reduce the intrusiveness of the nightmare. Krakow (2004) believes that IRT is not an exposure therapy, though he concedes that there is some exposure embedded within it. The treatment is available as a 4-hour CD series or as a digital download from the website www.nightmaretreatment.com, intended for either client or therapist. It has also been described as a 'creation' imagery technique by Hackmann et al. (2011), and the principles have been included in their recent book on working cognitively with imagery. The basic technique of changing the nightmare and then practicing the new dream is similar to some of the nightmare interventions described in Chapter 6.

Steps for the Therapist to follow when working with IRT

1 Select a disturbing dream, preferably one of a lesser intensity and not a re-enactment of a trauma.
2 Change this nightmare in any way you wish.
3 Rehearse this new dream for a few minutes every day.
4 Continue these instructions every day and consider working with another nightmare to change it into a new dream such that only one or two dreams are rehearsed each week.

Hackmann et al. (2011) describe some of the characteristics of IRT, including initially providing a period of psycho-education about dreams and nightmares, which help to improve treatment compliance. Clients are asked to create a written narrative of their nightmare in a rescripted form. Clients can either change the nightmare at any point they wish or change the ending. In general it might be helpful for the rescripted dream to have a positive-feeling tone, and increased mastery in the new account has been found to be important (Germain et al., 2004). Clients are asked to rehearse the rescripted nightmare on a daily basis.

EXAMPLE

Jamie had served in Northern Ireland and was suffering from PTSD. He was already in treatment with a colleague when he was referred for specific help with disturbing and intrusive dreams. He identified two dreams in particular. In the first one he was patrolling a road in Ireland with a colleague, when they were surprised and set upon by some men who had appeared from behind a building. Jamie managed to escape but his colleague was badly beaten. In the second dream Jamie was on the scene where a car bomb had exploded and he saw the badly mutilated driver being taken from the vehicle. In the third dream Jamie is asleep in his bedroom when he hears sounds of men approaching down the corridor outside his room. He is terrified that they are coming for him. He wakes as the door opens. Delia asked Jamie which was the least horrific, since it is suggested that treatment starts with a dream of lesser intensity. Jamie chose the dream of men approaching down the corridor, as this was not in fact a repeat of something that had actually happened. After providing Jamie with some information about dreams and nightmares, Delia discussed with Jamie how to rescript his dream and asked him to produce a written account. Jamie produced the following account:

> I'm in my room sleeping when I hear sounds of people approaching down the corridor; I quickly arm myself with a cricket bat so that I am ready for them. But as the sounds get closer, I realize that it is my friends coming back from a night out. I open the door and call out to them and we all come back into my room for a nightcap.

Delia asked Jamie to rehearse his rewritten dream each night before he went to bed. The following week he reported that he had not had that dream again. After his success Jamie felt able to tackle rescripting the first of his true post-traumatic dreams. In the weeks that followed, Jamie reported that his nightmares had significantly lessened in intensity and frequency and, though he still had some disturbing dreams about his time in Northern Ireland, he felt much more in control and empowered to work with them.

A similar but more structured form of intervention is exposure, relaxation and rescripting therapy (EERT), developed by Davis (2009). This three-session intervention involves, in the first session, psycho-education about trauma, nightmares and sleep habits, and progressive muscle relaxation. Homework practice in modifying bad sleep habits and practicing relaxation is given. The second treatment session involves rescripting the nightmare with homework to rehearse the rescripted nightmare. The third session reviews progress and discusses maintenance and relapse prevention. Therapists can find this more elaborated method detailed in Davis (2009).

As indicated earlier, IRT was initially developed for survivors of abuse, and the next section provides some suggestions when working with survivors of abuse.

Working with survivors of abuse

Some people who have suffered abuse will have symptoms of PTSD, including post-traumatic nightmares. These can be treated, alongside regular therapy, using the same interventions for nightmares that have already been described both in this chapter and in Chapter 6. Both IRT and eye movement, desensitisation and reprocessing (EMDR) can also be helpful where there are trauma symptoms. While Gestalt dreamwork techniques can be useful in encouraging the sufferer to confront their perpetrator, in my own work I don't encourage the sufferer to change chairs and take on or 'become' the perpetrator when working with sufferers of childhood sexual abuse. While it is true that Gestalt is primarily about intrapersonal splits and many sufferers may well have internalized their aggressor, personally I don't feel that it is appropriate for sufferers to take on the role of perpetrator in this work.

Some clients may present for therapy and may not have disclosed their abuse. It is possible for the abuse to be disclosed, and even brought into awareness, through the nightmares. The presence of significant childhood amnesia and/or psychogenic breathing difficulties may alert the therapist to this possibility. However, where the abuse is first brought into awareness through nightmares, the therapist must also be alert to the possibility of false memory syndrome and proceed cautiously. Where the abuse has not previously been disclosed in therapy, the client may well first disclose to the therapist through bringing their dreams. Sometimes the client feels safer, distanced from the abuse, and less ashamed by presenting in this way. The therapist can then work with the abuse through working through the nightmares as well as encouraging the client to talk about it directly.

In the first of the two examples that follow, my colleague, who is an eye movement desensitization and reprocessing (EMDR) practitioner, has worked with his client using EMDR interventions to successfully resolve his nightmares. EMDR is a specialist intervention not to be undertaken by anyone without appropriate training. Nevertheless, it is included here to demonstrate a different method of exposure and rescripting of the nightmare. In this case, the therapist does not give explicit instructions to his client to rescript the nightmare but, interestingly, this is what appears to happen naturally. It is as if the preliminary grounding and the EMDR facilitated this client to become empowered to rescript his nightmares in a more positive way.

EXAMPLE

John is a 60-year-old year man who sought help because of recurring nightmares which had plagued him since childhood. He had also struggled with anxiety and depression to varying degrees throughout his life, but this had been significantly alleviated by therapy and medication. His childhood was characterized by parental neglect, emotional and physical abuse, and he was repeatedly sexually abused by a family friend from the ages of 3 to 7. His parents left him in the care of various relatives for several months at a time during his childhood, and he was taken into local authority care for two years where he suffered further mistreatment.

In his recurring nightmares John is always lost and alone; often he is on a train or at a railway station. It is usually at night-time and it's raining. Often he is a child of 9 or 10, but even when he has an adult body in the dream he still feels like a young child. John is always preoccupied with finding his way home, but either there is no one else on the train or if there are other passengers they seem threatening and he is too afraid to speak to them and cannot orientate himself. Looking out of the train window the unfamiliar streets are dark and foreboding; sometimes he sees movement in shadows and is too frightened to get off the train. The dominant emotions are fear and loneliness. John has never found his way home or resolved the dream in any way, and he usually wakes up feeling frightened and disorientated. He often reports intrusive memories and flashbacks from these dreams in waking life.

Initially, treatment consisted of psycho-education about dreams and John kept a dream diary. This enabled him to feel more comfortable thinking about and discussing his dreams. He then learned some grounding exercises to help reorient him when waking from dreams or experiencing flashbacks. The grounding exercises included coping statements about being an adult, having strength/power and so on to counteract feelings of hopelessness and helplessness. This work improved his confidence and he began preparation for EMDR treatment by learning and practicing a 'safe place' exercise. John became very proficient at visualizing his safe place (sitting in his conservatory with his cats) and found this effective at soothing himself whenever he felt distressed.

John completed two EMDR sessions to address the same target image (lost, sitting on a deserted train at night, and looking out the window at the rain). This was associated with the negative cognition 'I don't know where I am' and he wanted to believe the positive cognition 'I am safe where I am'. He found this image very frightening (subjective units of distress (SUDS) 9 out of 10). During the EMDR several channels of association were explored. Thematically these included being physically punished, being taken to the home of the man who sexually abused him, and several other frightening memories – of the dark, being lost, and approached by menacing dogs. In each instance he was able to reach safety or received help and support, and felt more empowered. Examples include 'feeling braver' and going into the next carriage where supportive people tell him where to get off the train; a caring aunt preventing his mother from beating him, or shooing away the dogs; or being cleaned, dressed and comforted by another caring relative. Following the EMDR protocol he would then return to the target image to process further channels of association.

John then found the nightmares became less frequent, and for the first time in years he slept for four consecutive nights with no nightmares. He reported a corresponding reduction in intrusive memories when awake. Some nights he could not recall any dreams, had normal dreams or found the nightmares were more fleeting and less frightening. He also reported more dreams involving other childhood memories involving abuse or abandonment, but did not find these as frightening or overwhelming as the recurring nightmare. John continues with his treatment.

In the next example, Sharon was working with another colleague. Although the abuse was known about, and was the reason for the referral, Sharon did not feel able to talk about the abuse directly in the room. However, she did have constant nightmares of the abuse and the therapist encouraged Sharon to write them down and bring them to therapy. The dreams got more explicit as therapy progressed.

EXAMPLE

1 'I'm in my bedroom on my own. I have a sharp razor and I've cut my arms and legs. I'm looking at what I've done and cut the words "slut" and "slag" into my arm.'
2 'I'm with my mother, brother and sister in a house somewhere. I'm trying to clean up but they keep making more of a mess. I'm angry and I start shouting that Dad has been "screwing" me. But they just look at me and don't say anything. I'm trying desperately to clean up but they keep undoing everything I've done.'
3 'I'm shouting at Mum and asking her why she didn't do anything. She tells me that I'm just as bad and disgusting as he is.'
4 'Dad came into my room and I pretended to be asleep. He came over to the bed and raped me, telling me it's because you told.'
5 'Dad brings two men in with him and he is encouraging them to have sex with me. I try to hide but Dad catches me and I'm struggling and crying. He tears my clothes off and rapes me. The men are laughing and then Dad urges the men to do the same. They both rape me and it hurts and I'm crying.'

(Continued)

(Continued)

These nightmares are very explicit and they are a way of the client communicating what she wants without talking about the abuse directly. Sharon wanted to leave the written accounts with the therapist but was not comfortable to talk directly about the abuse or even to work with the nightmares in therapy. However, Sharon did make a lot of progress in therapy and the nightmares greatly reduced. It seemed that the very act of writing down the nightmares and giving them to the therapist was a way for Sharon to 'exorcise' them and get rid of them. As Sharon spoke about her dreams, she began to feel able to speak to her therapist about her abuse. However, she found this very distressing and so they continued to focus on the dreams. Although the therapist would have preferred to have worked more directly in the room with the abuse material, working in this way was somewhat effective for Sharon, who was not yet ready to do further exploratory work. Therapists need to be able to work flexibly and sensitively with nightmares and to take their cue from their clients.

Night terrors

This last section of the chapter describes another sleeping disturbance which can also cause intense distress to a few, though not all, of its sufferers, but about which relatively little is known. This is the phenomenon of 'night terrors', sometimes also known as 'sleep terrors'. A night terror is a sudden arousal from slow-wave sleep, non-rapid eye movement (NREM) stages 3 or 4, usually early in the night. It consists of a simple awakening in terror, most often accompanied by a scream, by sweating, by body movements, and sometimes by sleep-walking. The event usually lasts for one to several minutes before the person goes back to sleep, and during this time there are tremendous increases in autonomic nervous system activity. For example, pulse and breathing rates might double. Generally, however, although night terrors can be frightening to witness, the sleeper does not remember the night terror as they might a dream. There is usually no recall and an individual is only aware of the episode because they are told about it the next morning. If there is any recall, it usually consists of a single frightening image, usually choking or being suffocated. It is important not to confuse night terrors with nightmares, since treatment for the two conditions are very different. A night terror is not a dream, but the unusual awakening itself. This arousal, which includes rapid changes in the nervous system, and which may include movement and sleep-walking, is the night terror. It is therefore generally known as a disorder of arousal.

Night terrors are most commonly seen in young children between the ages of three and about seven. They are slightly more common in boys and are reported to occur in up to 4 per cent of children. Attacks may be weeks apart or may occur every night for a short spell and then abate for a while. Children nearly always grow out of them as they approach adolescence, if not before, and they are not generally a serious problem. Hartmann (1984) comments that, when night terrors begin in adolescence or in adulthood, they may be secondary to other factors, and are often chronic. There is a tendency for night terrors to run in families and some children may have a genetic predisposition to them. In children they are generally considered to be a minor abnormality of the arousal system. Mostly no treatment is required, since children grow out of them spontaneously and they are not linked to any psychological disturbance. Sometimes, however, in susceptible children, they can be aggravated by sleep deprivation, extreme tiredness, high temperatures or stress. Thus it may be helpful for parents to maintain a regular sleep schedule for their child and to attempt to reduce any particular stressors. Since night terrors are relatively common in children, it is worth discussing in more detail (in the section that follows) how therapists might help parents of children presenting with night terrors.

When night terrors continue into adulthood, or have their onset in adolescence or adulthood, they are still not necessarily linked to any medical or psychological difficulty. However, they may occasionally be a precursor to temporal lobe epilepsy, or they may follow a brain injury, or be linked to an abuse of alcohol or drugs. Some workers have commented that sufferers may be people who find it difficult to express strong feelings, notably anger, while awake. This has led to the notion that, for some people, night terrors may express a breakthrough of suppressed emotion.

Night terrors in adults are not usually either serious or dangerous. However, where they are linked to sleep-walking (somnambulism), which is also a disorder of NREM slow-wave sleep, there can be a danger that the sufferer may accidentally injure themselves. Indeed, there have been reports of accidents such as people falling from windows, or through glass, or even being involved in traffic accidents, while sleep-walking.

In terms of treatment, there are some fairly obvious issues for the therapist to consider. For example, the therapist might suggest making the surroundings safe for sleep-walkers. It is also worth checking for excessive drug and alcohol consumption, sleep deprivation and stressful situations. There is no clear evidence that either psychological therapy or medication will necessarily be helpful for either night terrors or sleep-walking. However, counselling or short-term psychotherapy may be helpful for some clients. The therapist might give the client basic information about the phenomena of night terrors and sleep-walking. Therapy might help the client to consider particular anxieties or stresses in their life and strategies for ameliorating them. It may also be helpful for the therapist to help the client to ventilate their feelings and to find appropriate ways of expressing difficult feelings, such as anger, in waking life. Where therapy is not helpful the therapist may want to refer the client for medical help. Medication has also sometimes been successful in the short term. However, there is usually a recurrence of the problem once the medication is withdrawn. Since night terrors are most frequently seen in children, some suggestions are presented below for therapists to help parents of young children.

Advice for the therapist when working with parents of children who have night terrors

Initially, it is important to know whether the situation presented is a night terror or a nightmare. Patricia Garfield, in her book *Your Child's Dreams* (1984), suggests a list of signs that will help distinguish between the two.

Indicators of night terrors

1   The child awakens suddenly with a piercing scream.
2   The child cries, moans or mumbles incoherently.
3   The child appears terrified or in pain.
4   The child sits up, jumps out of bed, or runs around. The attack is often followed by a sleep-walking episode.
5   The child's eyes are open, but staring and unseeing. The pupils may dilate and the child may hallucinate.
6   The child's heartbeat is racing (maybe double the normal rate).
7   The child perspires profusely.
8   The child breathes quickly and shallowly. They may gasp for breath.
9   The child remains agitated for several minutes, possibly up to half an hour, but may then fall asleep again relatively easily.
10   The child is not able to be consoled until the attack is over.
11   The child has been asleep for only about an hour and a half. (Two-thirds of all episodes occur early in the night during the first period of slow-wave sleep.)
12   The child is most likely to have night terrors between the ages of three and six, although they can occur at any age.
13   The child has little or no recall. Any memory is likely to be a single frightening image.
14   The child has no recollection of the attack in the morning.

If the child exhibits three or more of these signs, they probably have night terrors. If parents are shown the list they can usually distinguish their child's experience easily as night terrors, in contrast to the Garfield's (1984) list of signs of ordinary nightmares.

Indicators of nightmares

1   The child wakes upset, crying and frightened.
2   The child rarely emits piercing screams.
3   The child is frightened or anxious, but not terror struck or in panic.
4   The child may make movements, but does not fling themselves about.
5   The child does not perspire.

---

6   The child recalls a bad dream, often in detail, perhaps of a wild animal or monster in pursuit.
7   The child may confuse dream and reality somewhat, but they are coherent and not hallucinatory.
8   The child may have difficulty describing their feelings and fears.
9   The child realizes that the dream caused them to wake up.
10 The child responds to efforts to reassure and calm.
11 The child has been asleep for some time, about half the night.
12 The child is most likely to have nightmares between the ages of 7 and 10, although they can occur at any age.
13 The child mostly still recalls the nightmare in the morning.

If the child has three or more of the above indicators, they have probably just had a nightmare. It can be seen from the list of signs of night terrors that they are generally more dramatic and extreme than nightmares, and they are certainly unnerving to witness. Thus, parents may be frightened themselves and may think that something is seriously, psychologically wrong with their child. Probably the most helpful thing that the therapist can do is to educate and reassure the parents. This is extremely important, since parents may try inappropriate treatments or seek medication. Also, parents' concern will be communicated to the child, who may well become worried themselves. Occasionally parents have attached a label, such as 'hyperactive', to their child. This can then begin to create problems for the child.

When parents are frightened, they may even try to shake, slap or yell at their child in an attempt to rouse them. Therapists can therefore give parents suggestions for managing night terrors.

Suggestions for managing night terrors

1   Be available and protective, especially if the child is sleep-walking.
2   Do not attempt to forcibly restrain or hold the child, unless this is essential for safety, since restraint may intensify the attack.
3   Do not become angry or attempt to rouse the child by shaking, slapping or yelling.
4   Try to touch the child lightly if possible. Maybe put an arm around the child or stroke them soothingly.
5   Stay with the child and walk with them if they move about.
6   Speak calmly and reassuringly, even if the child does not appear to hear. Say 'You're OK now', 'I'm here', 'It's all right', 'It's all over' or other reassuring words.
7   A warm facecloth gently wiped over the child's face may help recovery.
8   Let the child go back to sleep again as soon as possible, and with the minimum of fuss.

The therapist can reassure parents that there is probably nothing seriously wrong with the child, that they are not injured or in pain, and that they have no recollection of the event; nor is the child likely to be worried about the night terror themselves, unless they have picked up their parents' anxiety. The therapist should reassure parents that night terrors are thought to be symptomatic of an 'immature nervous system' and are almost always outgrown.

EXAMPLE

Jason, who was eight, was brought along by his parents, who were extremely concerned that he was disturbed, mostly because of the horrifying nightmares that he was having with increasing frequency, but also because, recently, teachers had commented that Jason seemed distracted at school. Jason himself had not been particularly worried initially, but was beginning to think that there might be something wrong with him. In fact, on closer scrutiny, Jason's 'nightmares' turned out to be night terrors. Delia explained about the phenomenon and reassured Jason and his parents that the night terrors did not necessarily indicate any particular psychological or medical difficulty. She also gave them some tips (outlined above) for managing the attacks. Jason was seen individually for a couple of sessions and taught some methods of relaxation, since he sometimes had problems getting to sleep. When Delia asked Jason's parents if there were any particular pressures in Jason's life, they explained that Jason's father, who was a fireman, was getting increasingly stressed because of his work, and his extreme moodiness was causing rows at home. The couple were given about four sessions of therapy in which they were able to talk about their difficulties. They decided that Jason's father would change his job and that his mother would work part-time in order to help make up for the drop in the family's income.

At the end of therapy, about eight weeks altogether, Jason and his family reported that the night terrors were not really a problem any more. It appeared that they had reduced in frequency, and the occasional one that Jason did have did not unduly concern the family. Jason was also sleeping better and seemed 'back to his old self' at school. His parents were also acting on the family decisions that they had made and the whole family seemed considerably less tense. It is possible that the night terrors might have abated anyway, but it is probable that the drop in family stress levels, Jason's improved sleeping patterns, and the ability of Jason's parents to manage his night terrors, all had an influence.

Summary

A brief description of post-traumatic stress disorder (PTSD) is followed by a discussion and examples of acute and chronic post-traumatic nightmares. A model for chronic nightmare development and maintenance is presented followed by suggestions for treatment of post-traumatic nightmares. The main intervention of imagery rehearsal therapy (IRT) is outlined as well, as a related but more structured form of approach entitled exposure, relaxation and rescripting therapy (EERT). This is followed by suggestions for, and two examples of, working with survivors of abuse. Finally, night terrors are discussed and guidelines for working with children with night terrors are outlined.

8

Group and Creative Methods in Dreamwork

In this chapter some of the techniques for working with dreams in group settings are described. The group aspects of working with dreams are focused on by suggesting two important ways in which group contributions can enrich the process of interpretation. First, the group members can elaborate the actual dream material in ways that provide fresh insights for the dreamer. Second, one person's dream can provide insights for other members of the group. Initially, suggestions to the therapist for structuring group feedback will be outlined, and there is also an illustrative example. Some ways of working with dreams in a group, including psychodrama and sculpting, are then outlined.

Structuring group feedback

Any of the techniques described so far in this book can be used in group settings. The steps to be carried out are the same as those described for the one-to-one setting but, in addition, the therapist needs to facilitate the contributions of group members by ensuring that they are made in an appropriate manner. Group members' contributions can be made at different points in the dreamwork process. During the dreamwork the therapist can encourage group members to make suggestions or to ask clarifying or thought-provoking questions. These are most helpfully made when the dreamer appears to be stuck, for example, when attempting to work out the meaning of a particular symbol. At the end of the dreamer's work the group members can then share their ideas and feelings about the work that has taken place. This is most helpfully done by sharing personal reactions, particularly how the dream relates to their own lives. This provides mutual support for both dreamer and group member. It also allows the group members to relate aspects of the dream symbols or feelings to their own lives and to acknowledge their own feelings.

Perhaps the most important thing for the therapist to remember is that the dream belongs to the dreamer. This is especially critical in groupwork because of the tendency of the group members to swamp the dreamer with their own views. The following is a list of practical hints for the therapist.

Guidelines for the therapist to follow when structuring group dreamwork

1 The role of the dreamer is to listen to members' contributions, to select relevant ideas and to reject those that don't seem helpful.
2 Group members need to couch their comments in language that acknowledges their ownership of the contribution. For example, 'The red flag in your dream suggests danger to me' rather than 'The red flag in your dream means danger'.
3 The therapist should discourage group members from pressing the dreamer to delve deeper into the material than they want.
4 The therapist should also ensure that the dreamer is not pressured into disclosing more personal material than they choose. The therapist can check for signs of discomfort and intervene to prevent over-insistent questioning, as well as reminding the dreamer that they can stop at any point. Sometimes it is possible for group members to feel frustrated because they have not fully understood the meaning of the dream. However, it may be helpful to remind people that the purpose of dreamwork is that the dream should make sense for the dreamer.
5 The impact of working with dreams can be very powerful, and dreamers may be caught unawares by the strength of their reaction. Therefore, the therapist must be prepared for the fact that what may seem to the dreamer like a very innocuous dream can quickly lead them into deep personal material. The therapist needs to be comfortable working with the material that is presented and should also be careful not to encourage the dreamer to work with material that is too overwhelming.
6 Therapists should discourage questioning, except for the purposes of clarification. In particular 'why' questions lead the dreamer away from the actual dream experience and into post hoc rationalizations. Questions can easily turn the whole process into an inquisition, which is rarely therapeutic. Rather, the therapist can encourage group members to share personal statements and feelings in the form of 'I' statements.
7 It is not only the dreamer who can become vulnerable when the disguised nature of the dream material begins to be uncovered. Other group members may be similarly affected by their own associations to the dream material, and this can be true whether they have actually spoken during the session or not. It is therefore important for the therapist to check that members are able to contain the feelings aroused in the group, or that they have an identified form of support to which they can turn.

EXAMPLE

This example of structuring group feedback occurred in a dream workshop. The feedback came after Maureen had been working on her dream using the Gestalt method. Since the object of this example is to illustrate the feedback aspect, the account of Maureen's dream and the associated work has been summarized. The following is the essence of what Maureen told us of her dream:

> She was sitting on a bed, in a room, looking young like her daughter, and feeling lost and sad. Sitting next to her was an older, shadowy version of herself. Her critical parents were standing in the room looking at her. In the dream Maureen was looking out of a patio window, and was watching helplessly as her ex-husband's wife pushed Maureen's car over a cliff. Maureen asked her father for help, which he refused. She next saw her daughter struggling with her father (Maureen's ex-husband) in the water. Maureen again asked her father for help and he refused again. She felt despair.

Maureen then repeated the dream, choosing to tell it from the points of view of her father, her daughter in the water, her car and the window, respectively.

Father: I like the stronger part of my daughter I can see sitting on the bed. I don't like the forlorn one. I'll only help my daughter when she's strong. I can see the car going over the cliff, but my daughter has to help herself. I see her daughter struggling and my daughter is asking for help, but she's very selfish, always making demands on me. I've done my bit.

Daughter: I can see my mother looking horrified at her car being pushed over the cliff. My father is responsible for this and I'm angry with him. I'm also angry that Mum is horrified about the car and not about me, but now I see that she's also upset and horrified about me being in the water and fighting with my father.

Car: I'm fairly old and neglected, but my owner is very proud of me. I don't want to be pushed over the cliff, but I'm powerless.

Window: I see a lot happening, but there's nothing I can do. I feel stuck.

Delia then asked Maureen who she would like to 'talk to' using the Gestalt 'empty chair' method. Maureen chose her father:

Maureen: Why wouldn't you help me? You could see my car being destroyed, and Sasha in the water. I needed your help and you wouldn't help me at all! [*Maureen spoke in a low monotone.*]

Father: I've been a good father. You're always asking for help. I've done everything I can to help you. You're grown up now. I'm sick and tired of you!

(Continued)

(Continued)

> You're always getting yourself into a mess and expecting us to bail you out. Mother and I have got our own lives to lead. Stand on your own two feet!

Maureen: You've not been a good father. You've made my childhood unhappy. You've only given me material things. You don't love me. You reject my children. I want you to love me. [*Maureen still spoke in a low, controlled voice.*]

At Delia's invitation, Maureen expressed more angry feelings towards her father and became quite emotional. Maureen continued:

Maureen: You've caused me lots and lots of problems in my life. You've made me feel worthless. You've made me feel in the way between you and Mum, which has caused me lots of problems with relationships in my life. I hate you for thinking that you're a good father, when you haven't been! I'm sick of you treating me like a child!

At this point Maureen became very emotional and chose to stop working.

Delia invited members of the group to contribute. She asked them to share what was going on for them while Maureen was working and to say what they felt. She suggested a structure of 'When you said ... I felt ...'. At first there was a pause, which was broken by Maggie speaking very softly:

Maggie: I felt very sorry for you.

Delia: Did it remind you of any feelings of your own?

Maggie: It brought up the situation with my father. We were never very close.

Penny: [*Choking back tears*] I felt it reminded me of my father. He also gave me material things, but he didn't help me with my relationship with my mother. I was very angry with him and I was fighting back tears when you were working.

Freda: I feel very sad.

Angela: I felt very sorry for you. I knew what the outcome would be. The window isn't just stuck. It's your other vision. You should help yourself. You don't need them to help. [*She spoke in a high-pitched, angry voice.*]

Delia asked Angela to 'own' her statement.

Angela: I felt that for me, the window was your other vision. [*After a slight pause, in a lower voice*] I felt frustrated because I feel you are capable of doing things for yourself. Maybe it reminds me of how I used to be.

Freda: I identified with the car. But for me, my car represents freedom. Your car was stuck, so was the window and the bed, all stuck! My feeling is 'help!' It's about my feeling of being stuck myself.

Rita:	[*Agitated and angry*] You chose the wrong man in your dream . . .
Delia:	[*Prompting Rita*] Can you make a statement for you?
Rita:	For me, if I'd have been in your dream, I'd have spoken to the ex-husband. You were just putting blame on your father where it shouldn't be. You didn't show any sympathy for your father. You didn't try to understand him . . .
Delia:	[*Interrupting Rita*] Rita, I know this seems hard to do. But it is important not to make judgements, give advice, or to try to change what Maureen has said about her dream. It is more helpful if you can share with the group the relevant aspects of your *own* experience and feelings.
Rita:	[*Angry*] My father was typical of his generation. He was never emotionally expressive. I've tried my best to understand him. It was just his way. He didn't not love me.
Kelly:	When I was a child my father seemed so huge and so powerful. He was loving but he dominated me. As I've grown up we've become more equal and I get on with him fine now.
Freda:	Can I ask you, Maureen, what were your feelings about the car being pushed over? Did you want to rescue it?
Delia:	Freda, try to make a statement about your own feelings, rather than asking a question.
Lynn:	[*Intervening*] I felt strongly about the car. I feel that I, myself, don't have the power to do things for myself.
Ruth:	[*Agitatedly*] For me, I'd have wanted to talk to the window. For me, it's a block preventing me from getting to the car or the daughter.
Maggie:	For me the window was a divider. It divided the inside from what was going on outside.
Freda:	But I was aware of sadness in the scene inside and the scene outside.
Maureen:	Can I come in here? I think I understand that the inside scene represents the inside bit of me and the outside scene represents the external part of me. The daughter in the water was really me and I was battling with my ex-husband. The dream brings the two parts of me together.
Chloe:	A lot for me in the dream is about being an adult in my body, but inside being a helpless and confused child, and other people expecting me to behave like an adult. When I heard your father saying 'Stand on your own feet', I thought that's fine and dandy! But I wish I'd been equipped to do it. [*She started crying.*]

(Continued)

(Continued)

The group continued to work for some time on the theme of 'stuckness', which had emerged as a theme for some group members, though not for Maureen herself. But mostly the sharing concerned relationships with fathers, which was Maureen's main issue. This was crystallized by Chloe's comments and show of emotion, which resonated profoundly for most of the group members.

It is necessary for the therapist to *manage* the group feedback, and they often have to be quite directive in getting participants to keep to an appropriate format. If these guidelines are followed, the work of the dreamer, as well as other group members, is facilitated.

Dreamwork techniques for working in groups

In this section, three ways of working with dreams in groups are presented. These are 'If this were my dream', psychodrama and sculpting.

'If this were my dream'

This is a popular and helpful way of working with dreams in groups and is particularly useful in building up group trust and cohesion. It is also a good way of bringing a group together after individual work or at the end of a workshop. This exercise encourages anybody to join in, and to contribute in a creative rather than an analytical manner. Essentially, a group member offers a dream, which is then taken on board by the other group members as if it were their dream. Finally, the dreamer re-owns the dream. A version of this exercise has been reported by Ullman and Zimmerman (1983), although it has also been used by others. The somewhat modified steps, as described by Shohet (1985), are given below.

Guidelines for the therapist to follow when using 'If this were my dream'

1 The therapist asks for a volunteer to recount a dream. It is advisable to select a dream that is relatively short so that the group does not get lost in too much detail. The dream also needs to be fairly recent, so that the dreamer is in touch with relevant, waking happenings (day residue). It is important to select a dream that hasn't already been interpreted by the dreamer, so that a genuine unfolding may take place.

2 The dreamer recounts the dream, in the first person, present tense. While they are doing this, other group members listen to the dream and imagine that it is their own dream that is being recounted. It is usually helpful for the dreamer to recount the dream a second time. After this the group members may ask

---

questions about content only. These questions should be for the purpose of clarification, in order to fill in any necessary details to help participants imagine the dream as their own. For example, 'When you reached the seashore, was it daytime or night-time?' or 'Were there other people sitting on the bus with you?'. The group should avoid questions about the dreamer's processing, such as 'How did you feel when you saw the child?'. The therapist should help the group not to get carried away asking too many specific details, since this can prevent them from entering into the fantasy of the dream.

3 At this point the therapist invites the dreamer to become an observer and to listen to the proceedings, as well as taking notes if she wishes.

4 The therapist then asks the group members to identify the feelings in the dream as if it were their own dream, using the structure 'In my dream I felt ...'. It is not a good idea for the therapist to go round the group. We usually find that most members will wish to make at least one statement, but there is no obligation to say anything or to speak only once. This is an exercise where the therapist can also make a contribution if she wishes.

5 When no more statements are forthcoming, the therapist invites the members to go beyond the feelings into the dream itself, using the structure 'If this were my dream'. Members can take up the dream and expand or change it in any direction. It is important to keep to the 'If this were my dream' format to ensure that everybody is clear that they are dealing with their own projections and not imposing meanings onto another person's dream.

6 When this stage has been completed, the dreamer is invited to comment. They may like to say which statements have 'resonated' with them, but they are under no obligation to comment on all or even any of the statements. The dreamer is invited to relate the dream to anything relevant that is happening in their life, but again is under no obligation to do so. It is important for the dreamer to feel that they can re-own their dream at this stage as well as to let them make their own connections without others forcing suggestions onto them.

7 Group members are then invited to share personal feelings or thoughts about any aspects of the exercise, either about the dream or about other member's comments that have resonated for them. This can often be a particularly rich part of the exercise. We have found that it is very common, at this stage, for a universal theme to have emerged from the dream, and a common occurrence is a sharing of members' different ways of dealing with this. However, it is by no means certain that a universal theme will emerge. Quite often two or three distinct themes or interpretations are identified, and this can also lead to fruitful group sharing of experiences.

EXAMPLE

Robyn worked with Carol on her dream, focusing on the group aspects:

I'm aged about nine or ten in the dream, although I'm fairly big and muscular. It's Sunday evening and I'm sitting with my parents in the living room of our house. Suddenly, three manholes appear in the carpet and three huge

(Continued)

(Continued)

crocodiles emerge from them and stand on their back legs. My parents just start shrinking, they become small and wizened. That's it.

After following steps 2 and 3 described above, Robyn asked group members to tell their feelings using the structure 'In my dream I felt'. The following feelings were expressed by members of the group:

In my dream I felt . . .

scared, but angry my parents are disappearing and not helping. . . . it's up to me to kill the crocodiles. ... I must protect my parents.

I would look for help. My parents are pathetic as usual, I must protect myself.

The crocodiles aren't really ferocious.

I have to look after myself. I'm frightened but fascinated.

I hate being strong.

I'm annoyed with the crocodiles. We were going to watch a film.

I'm glad I'm strong.

I find the crocodiles filthy and disgusting.

When no more responses were forthcoming, Robyn asked the group to move on a stage if they wished, and expand on their previous statements, using the format:

If this were my dream . . .

I'd tell them to clear off, and they do.

I'd make my parents stronger.

More crocodiles would appear.

My parents would just be bigger and stronger and deal with the crocodiles.

The crocodiles could be shrivelled up.

I'd follow the crocodiles down manholes and play with them. ... I'd block up the manholes.

I'd make the crocodiles into furry nice creatures, that were fun to be with.

I'd put the crocodiles back down the crocodile holes. They are not manholes they're crocodile holes.

I'd start to scream until my parents did something. The crocodiles would run away and I'd scream and scream. ... I'd jump out of the window. ... I'd be worried about the carpet!

Robyn next invited Carol to feed back to the group:

> The bit about parents not helping, and disappearing, really struck a chord with me. I've always had to deal with things myself. I feel some anger and disgust now that I didn't feel at the time. I don't like the feeling of being strong and having muscles. At the time I didn't understand it – I do now. I wanted my parents to be there to protect me. I liked it when you said 'I'd tell them to clear off'. Yes, get lost! [*laughter*] But I wouldn't like more to appear! [*more laughter*] Yes, I'd like my parents to deal with them and make them nice. It would be nice if I could deal with them, but I don't think I could. Manholes and crocodile holes? You mean put them where they belong? Yes, I like that idea. I liked the idea of screaming for help, yes. [*giggle*] Jumping out of the window wouldn't have solved anything but I'd have been out of the way. Worried about the carpet? [*hilarity*] No, I wouldn't have worried, but my mother would – silly Axminster carpet.

At this point Robyn invited the group to share their own feelings about the dream:

To me, I felt a reaction to a threatening situation was running away.

For me, it was more a feeling of helplessness. It reminded me of my parents. They should have been there for me, and they weren't.

I was just intrigued by the number of solutions that came up. I could only think of jumping out of the window. I would like to have been able to do something else. I don't do the right thing in a threatening situation. I was interested hearing other people's reactions.

It felt very claustrophobic – all the family there for tea. I remember those Sunday teas in my home when I was a child. The fact that someone else described it made it universal.

For me, the opposite was true. I felt that the peace of the family was intruded on. I wanted to watch telly.

Oh! I couldn't bear that. For me it was the opposite. The crocodiles saved me from an evening of boredom with the family.

The crocodiles would have been more disturbing to me if they had lounged around with the family.

At the end of the feedback Robyn invited Carol to re-own her dream. Carol explained that, although the dream occurred nine or ten years ago, it had stayed with her ever since. She had experienced a sense of liberation, hearing other people's feelings and reactions to her dream. She said she thought that she had finally 'laid the crocodiles to rest'.

It was suggested earlier that this exercise is usually best carried out with a recent dream, but this provides an example of how old dream material can also be worked on, since this particular dream had haunted Carol for many years. The reader will notice that no attempt was made during the exercise to pressure Carol into revealing more material than she chose.

Psychodrama

Before outlining steps in using these techniques with dreams, it is necessary to briefly describe psychodrama. Psychodrama is a form of group psychotherapy in which the person acts through their feelings in a structured situation, rather than just talking about them. J.L. Moreno (1987), who pioneered psychodrama, believed that true insight came from the cathartic experience of people expressing their feelings directly. There is no elaborate psychological theory of psychodrama, but Moreno believed that many of us have limited our behavioural repertoire and become rather stereotyped in our efforts to conform to the pressures of society. He believed that we have lost our ability to be 'spontaneous' and 'creative'. Moreno used these terms in particular ways, which are not easy to define, but 'spontaneity' is the capacity of the person to act in a free and relevant way, rather than being limited by stereotyped and possibly inappropriate responses. 'Creativity' is the person's inner energy giving rise to spontaneous behaviour. Moreno thought that when we behave and relate in a 'creative' and 'spontaneous' way there is the possibility of real communication, or what he called 'tele', between people.

Psychodrama can prepare people for more relevant and adaptive living by helping them to release blocked emotions, which in turn can lead to insight. Moreno's wife, Zerko Moreno, has called psychodrama 'a way of practicing living without being punished for making mistakes'. Psychodrama can be a very powerful way of bringing dreams to life and acting through the emotions contained in them. Again, this method can be difficult for an untrained facilitator. Information about training in Britain can be obtained from the British Psychodrama Association, which publishes the *British Journal of Psychodrama* and *Sociodrama*. Useful books on psychodrama are: *The Handbook of Psychodrama* (Karp, Holmes & Bradshaw, 1998), *A Clinician's Guide to Psychodrama* (Leveton, 2001) and *Acting In: Practical Applications of Psychodramatic Methods* (Blatner, 1973).

Guidelines for acting through dreams are given below.

Steps for the therapist to follow when working with psychodrama

1 The therapist, usually called in this method the 'director', chooses the 'protagonist', that is, the person whose dream is to be enacted.
2 The therapist asks the dreamer to tell the dream and to begin to show what happened in the dream by physically setting up the scene or 'stage'.
3 The therapist asks the dreamer to choose other group members, called in psychodrama 'auxiliary egos' or 'auxiliaries', to play the other characters or objects in the dream. The dreamer briefs the auxiliaries, sometimes by role-reversing with them in order to demonstrate the character and behaviour of the dream figures they are enacting.

4   When the action of enacting the dream begins, the therapist uses role reversal in order for the dreamer to identify with each of the dream figures.

5   At some point the dream climax will be reached. This is usually accompanied by an emotional release (which may be slight) and the dream insight or message will be clear to the dreamer.

6   At this point the dreamer may be content to end the acting through. However, the dreamer may want to act a different scene, for example, how they would have liked the dream to be different, or how they would have liked a different ending to the dream, or how they would like their life to be different from the dream.

7   The psychodrama ends with sharing. The auxiliaries and then group members, who are called in psychodrama the 'audience', take it in turns to share with the dreamer the feelings the dreamwork has aroused in them, and to express those aspects with which they have personally identified. This is a crucial part of the psychodrama for several reasons:

a   It allows the other group members to acknowledge their feelings, which are often very powerful.

b   It allows the auxiliary egos to de-role, which is essential.

c   It gives some recognition and support to the protagonist/dreamer.

EXAMPLE

Annette dreamed that:

she went to visit her friend, Paul, in hospital. She found herself walking down long corridors but was unable to find him. Nobody would tell Annette where she could find Paul. Finally she asked a group of nurses where she could find him. They said 'Up there.' Annette looked up and saw that there was a bed on top of some scaffolding. Paul was lying there in bed; he had his mouth open and his tongue was hanging out. Annette knew that Paul had AIDS. At the head of Paul's bed there was a man dressed all in white. He was standing with his arms crossed over his chest, slowly shaking his head. He was surrounded by a shining aura and his eyes and ears were covered in white bandages. On looking at Paul, Annette saw that he had blue marks all over him, which she recognized as the AIDS virus. Paul said 'Help me' and Annette held his hand. As she held his hand the blue marks began to transfer themselves onto Annette's hand and up her arm until there were no blue marks left on Paul. Annette said 'I'd better go now' and she started to leave. She found it difficult to get out of the hospital. She was holding her arm up and straight out so that people would see it was important that she got through. But people kept holding her back, delaying her and slowing her down. Annette was in a hurry to get out and get rid of the marks on her arm. Finally she got out of the hospital and the dream ended.

(Continued)

(Continued)

As Annette told her dream a second time, Delia (as director) asked Annette to show her what happened. Annette walked round with Delia and began to set up the scene. She placed some desks with chairs on top for scaffolding and she made a bed of cushions on top of the chairs. She chose a group member to play Paul; he was put in bed, covered by a blanket, and had some blue material draped over his arm to represent the AIDS virus. Annette chose another group member to be the man in white. He stood on a box on the 'scaffolding', at the head of the bed. He had a white coat around him and a white cardigan draped over his head. Annette also placed a number of group members in two lines to represent people who were slowing her down as she left the hospital. Annette briefed her 'auxiliaries'; this was not difficult, since so few words had actually been spoken.

As the action started, Annette moved towards the 'scaffolding' and climbed up. She moved to the bed:

> *Paul:* Help me! [*Annette took his hand.*]
>
> *Director:* What happened next?
>
> *Annette:* I want to know who this person in white is, who is so shining and untouchable and who doesn't seem to see what is happening here.
>
> *Director:* Well, ask him.
>
> *Annette:* Who are you?

The director immediately asked Annette to role-reverse with the man in white.

> *Annette:* I'm Mike and I don't want to know what's happening to Paul. I can't bear to see what's going on.

The director asked Annette to move back. She did so shaking her head angrily. As soon as they were in their original places the director briefed the auxiliary playing Mike to repeat Annette's words back to her.

> *Auxiliary as Mike:* I'm Mike and I just don't want to know what's going on here. I just can't bear to see what is happening to Paul. I just want to block it out.
>
> *Annette:* [*shouting*] You think you're so white and perfect and you just don't want to know! Look what's going on and stop avoiding things. You can't make things clean and tidy by not seeing the problems. I can't bear you to be so aloof and shut off! Stop protecting yourself and help Paul.

The director asked Annette what she wanted and she said to dismiss the man in white and carry on. Annette then told the man in white to go. She turned and held Paul's hand, as she did so transferring the blue cloth to her arm.

Annette: I'm going to leave now. I'm happy to carry the AIDS virus and take it out but I'm worried about the people getting in my way.

The director suggested that she leave, walking through the two lines of people. Annette pushed strongly through the two lines of people, telling them to get out of her way. At this point the action ended.

Many people were in tears and, in the sharing that followed, the director encouraged auxiliaries and group members to acknowledge the aspect of the dream with which they had most identified. A notable theme was the anger that some group members felt about partners and parents who were 'blinkered' and who were unwilling to communicate about what was really going on.

Angela: When my daughter was very ill in hospital, my husband just switched off. He didn't seem to want to know. I was the one who had to hold everything together. I've never really forgiven him for not being there when I needed him.

Ruth: Your scene reminded me of how I felt when I was in hospital. I felt like that man in the bed. My mother and husband would always argue, even in the hospital. I don't know if they even noticed me.

Derek: I feel very sad. I think I understand how Mike feels. I've lost someone and it's not very easy just to watch them going down hill. It's like you're losing them gradually. I think I switched off at times too. I feel bad about it now, but you have to go through it to know.

June: My situation isn't the same. I haven't lost anybody. But my partner seems to wear bandages over his eyes most of the time. I'm so angry that he doesn't really even seem to want to understand how I feel. I was so pleased when you shouted at him.

Cathy: I feel really angry. Really it's just the whole AIDS thing and people's reactions to it. There are tragedies all the time and a lot of people just don't want to know. I think it's the hypocrisy that makes me so mad.

The group members' involvement and their expressions of anger helped Annette to focus on her own anger towards Mike. Annette went on to explain that she felt relieved that she had identified the man in white as Paul's real-life partner who was being unsupportive towards Paul, who had recently been tested as HIV positive. She felt satisfied that she had told Mike what she thought and felt somewhat stronger for having pushed through the people on her way out. Annette had said that she had initially assumed that the dream had been about her trying to help Paul and had been surprised by how angry she felt towards Mike, Paul's partner.

Some time later Annette reported that, as a result of the dreamwork, she had confronted Mike about how she felt and had been able to support him and Paul to work through some of their feelings about the HIV diagnosis.

Readers may feel that there are many other rich symbols and issues in this dream that they would have liked to have seen explored further. However, it is the author's view that the therapist must follow the emotional direction of the client. In this case the dreamer was satisfied with the work that she did and was able to use the dreamwork in her waking life. Psychodrama was probably a more suitable technique than Gestalt for working on this dream, since it was, at this level of analysis anyway, a level 2 dream. That is, this dream put Annette strongly in touch with some unacknowledged feelings about a person in her current life. This connection with unacknowledged feelings can also be achieved by 'sculpting', the method to be described next.

Sculpting

There are many action methods related to psychodrama: one we have found helpful in working with dreams is 'sculpting'.

Steps for the therapist to follow when working with sculpting

1 The dreamer describes a particular dream scene and the therapist helps the dreamer to begin to get into the feelings by physically creating the setting. This may include props.

2 The dreamer chooses people from the group to represent the various characters and objects that will form the sculpture. They then sculpt the scene by physically placing the people in their correct positions as if they were 'human clay'. Often the sculptor may attempt to explain the meaning of the sculpture; at this point the sculptor should be encouraged to show rather than tell.

3 When the sculpture is complete the dreamer places themselves in it.

4 Each person in the sculpture then says one sentence: 'I'm [words describing physical position] and I feel ...'. An example might be 'I'm high up and I feel on top of the world' or 'I'm at the front and I feel exposed'. The therapist makes sure that words are kept to a minimum.

5 The therapist then asks the dreamer for their sentence.

6 The therapist asks the dreamer if there is one thing that they would like to change in the sculpture.

7 If a change is made then each of the people in the sculpture repeats a sentence from their new position. Examples might be 'I'm still high up and feel a bit shaky' or 'I'm not at the front now and I feel more supported'.

8 The dreamer shares their experiences and any insight gained.

9 Each of the people in the sculpture then shares their feelings and experiences with the dreamer, using the process to de-role. De-roling means making sure that the role-players have really managed to get fully out of role. The therapist

---

needs to ensure that all participants are de-roled by encouraging them to share their feelings about the role and, if necessary, by asking them directly if they feel fully out of role.

10 Other members of the group, who have not been in the sculpture, share their feelings and give feedback.

11 The dreamer reflects on the dream message and the meaning of this in their own life.

EXAMPLE

Jane described a dream in which the central feature was that she was riding on a roundabout horse at a fair. She was aware that other people were also riding on the roundabout but was unaware of who they were. In the dream she had felt a bit unsafe and confused. At this point Jane did not have any ideas about what the dream might be about and decided that she would like to try sculpting the scene.

Jane set up chairs in a circle to represent the roundabout and balanced two chairs rather precariously to represent her own roundabout horse. She then selected about eight people to sit on the other chairs and she placed herself on her wobbly horse. However, she did not find this satisfactory as it did not give her the rather dizzy feeling of movement she had felt in the dream. At this point she instructed the people to walk quickly round the circle of chairs, while she remained seated on her wobbly chairs.

Delia then asked the people in the sculpture to say one sentence:

Pat said 'I'm rushing past and I feel out of touch.'

John said 'I'm going too fast and I'm not going to wait.'

Chris said 'I'm going forward and I feel in control.'

Linda said 'I'm one of the crowd and I feel I can't stop.'

When each person had spoken Delia asked Jane how she was feeling. She said 'I'm being propelled along and I feel out of control.' She added that she was very surprised by the intensity of the feelings and that this had brought the dream feelings back to her.

Delia then asked Jane if there was one thing she wanted to change about the dream sculpture. Jane said she would like to stop the roundabout and get off. At this point Jane changed her rather indecisive demeanour and said 'Stop'. When the people stopped, Jane stepped down from the roundabout. At this point Delia asked the people in the sculpture to speak from their new positions:

John said 'I'm standing still and am frightened I won't get anywhere.'

Anthea said 'I'm standing still and I feel more grounded.'

(Continued)

(Continued)

Pat said 'I've stopped rushing and feel more in touch.'

Linda said 'I'm one of the group but I feel I can act independently.'

Jane said 'I'm not being pulled along and I feel in control.' She went on to describe how the meaning of the dream for her was to identify how she felt life was moving rather too fast for her. She had been promoted at work and moved house in the past three months. Her new position meant that she felt she had to work long hours and had to socialize with a lot of people from work; she no longer seemed to see old friends. She said that life did seem like a merry-go-round and that she had felt rather carried along by events and somewhat powerless. She felt that in order to actualize the dream she would have to take stock of her life and think about how she was going to make time to see important people in her life and feel more in control of things. Jane added that by going beyond the actual dream in the sculpting and stopping the roundabout she felt more empowered.

Group members shared their own feelings about the work that had been done and described similar experiences of their own. Jane felt supported and less isolated as she learnt about other people's experiences of feeling powerless at times during their lives. This encouraged Jane to explore her own feelings in more depth and to hear how others had coped with the problem. Linda explained how she had confronted her boss over a similar issue, and this gave Jane a degree of resolve to act similarly.

Of course, sculpting was not the only way to work with this dream. A merry-go-round is a powerful symbol and a cognitive approach might have worked equally well. One reason for suggesting sculpting was that Jane appeared distanced from the feelings in her dream and could not visualize it very strongly. This seemed a very vivid way of enabling Jane to contact the feelings in her dream. She was also willing to try this approach. One common problem when psychodrama or other action methods are suggested is that some people feel anxious or say that it won't work because they can't act. Acting skills are not necessary, but it usually helps to have some form of physical warm-up activity before using action methods. One very important point for the therapist to note is that action methods are very powerful and they must feel comfortable with, and able to contain, strong feelings. With both sculpting and psychodrama very powerful feelings can be put onto, or projected onto, characters in the sculpture or the drama. Hence it is important for the therapist to spend time allowing these feelings to be explored and dealing with any other unfinished business that may have occurred in the process. The sharing and de-roling are built into the process and should never be ignored. The author's experience is that the sharing and feedback process take at least as long as the original action and often far longer.

The chapter is concluded by presenting a number of creative dream group exercises. While these exercises can have a place in individual therapy, they are especially helpful when working with a dream group.

Converting the day into a dream

This group exercise is useful as a warm-up in a new group.

1 The therapist simply invites members to think of the day up until that point (or the day before if the group starts early in the day) as if it were a dream.
2 The therapist invites group members to note it down as a dream story or to draw it if they prefer.
3 The therapist then invites members to recount their story or talk about their drawing.

This exercise helps group members to deal with any 'unfinished business' and brings them into the 'here and now' by reviewing and letting go of outside affairs. The exercise can also provide a brief and light way of exchanging personal information and present preoccupations. Most importantly, this exercise can provide newcomers to the group with a way in to the fantasy world of dreams, highlighting some of the aspects of dream language and symbolism by working in reverse order. So the 'would-be' dreamworker moves from the conscious to a less conscious level by choosing some appropriate symbols to represent the real world, and by attempting to create something of the unusual and bizarre aspect of dream life. A variation on this exercise would be to ask group members to focus on one important aspect, theme or event of the day, to choose one or more symbols to represent this, and then to weave a fantasy story around the symbols.

Dream artwork

Painting and drawing can be a very relevant way to explore dreams, since dreams often consist of vivid imagery that cannot always be put into words. Of course, the imagery is such that few people would feel that they can do it justice in a painting. Nevertheless, drawing and painting has a place in dream therapy for individuals as well as for groups, since dream artwork can provide a private space for people to work creatively, and can therefore be an important alternative to verbal methods.

There are many imaginative exercises and therapists who like to work in this way can develop their own. Examples might be: asking dreamers to choose a symbol from each scene of the dream and to use these to make a design (e.g. a heraldic shield), possibly with a motto which is the dream message; to produce a group

(Continued)

(Continued)

drawing and identify group themes; to make clay or plasticine models; to produce written work such as individual or group stories or poems.

One simple format is simply to invite group members to make a pictorial representation of their dream. Dreamers are encouraged to portray a scene, mood, symbol or other aspect of their dream. They are encouraged not to focus on artistic skills but to use diagrams, line drawings, symbols or colours. Each person is invited to talk about their picture to the group. Members are then invited to question or comment. This can be a satisfying group activity focusing on dreams. It can have a number of valuable functions:

1   The opportunity to explain and discuss a picture can provide a way into the dream, which can be taken at any level the dreamer wishes. The therapist may suggest that the work could be followed up, for example, by using any of the subjective methods outlined in Chapter 5.
2   The dreamer is freed from any of the structural constraints of other methods and can focus on any aspect of the dream that interests them. This is essentially an approach taken from art therapy, with the focus on the subject of dreams.
3   The act of making a picture of a dream is in itself a satisfying activity, which can result in highly creative work as well as being a powerful bonding activity for a group.
4   The act of producing a 'dream product' can be helpful in allowing some way of closing the dreamwork when the dreamer has not been able to find a satisfactory resolution (or even when they have). It is especially helpful if the dream has been frightening or overwhelming.

It is usually helpful to end dream workshops with some form of 'creative exercise' in order to allow the dreamer a way of effecting closure on the work.

Fantasy exercise

This exercise is a way of encouraging members to disengage from the group while preparing them for continuing with their dreamwork on their own. The following is one of the group fantasies that I have used in my dream workshops, although the therapist might want to create their own that is particularly suitable to their purpose. It can be helpful to dim the lights and suggest that people find a relaxed position, preferably lying on the floor. People are instructed to follow the facilitator's suggestions if they find them comfortable, but if for any reason participants don't want to continue with the fantasy, they are told to tune-out the facilitator's voice. Since this exercise is used at the end of a workshop, its aim is to effect closure. However, occasionally someone has become upset during the exercise and may need a little support. This is a rare occurrence, and most group members find the fantasy enjoyable as well as being a comfortable way to end the workshop. The dots in the following suggested script represent places where the therapist might pause for a few seconds.

The fantasy

Find a comfortable position, lying on your back if possible. Close your eyes and become aware of your body . . . Turn your attention away from outside events and notice what is going on inside you . . . Become aware of all the details of your breathing . . . Feel the air move in through your nose and mouth . . . Feel it move down your throat . . . And feel your chest and stomach move as you breathe . . . Now imagine that your breathing is like gentle waves on the shore, and that each wave slowly washes some tension out of your body . . . and releases you even more . . . Your body feels very relaxed and heavy, as if it could sink into the floor . . . Stay breathing evenly and slowly and you feel even more relaxed . . . Now your body is beginning to feel lighter, and as you continue to relax you can feel your body becoming lighter still ... As you relax, your body feels so light that you imagine it starts to leave the ground . . . You imagine that you begin to float gently upwards and out of the room . . . Very gently you float steadily upwards and there is still, blue sky all around you . . . You become aware that you are lying on a warm, soft, fluffy cloud . . . You are aware of the countryside far below you and other clouds floating gently past you . . . You are still feeling very relaxed and content . . . Gradually you become aware that you are floating into another world ... It is your dream world ... As you begin to float in through the entrance you begin to meet your dreams ... At first they may seem white and flimsy, but as you continue through your dream world, they gradually begin to take shape . . . Your dreams are all around you as you move through them on your cloud . . . Stop and take a look at your dreams. Do you recognize any of them? . . . Now begin silently to talk to your dreams. Tell them how you have been feeling about them . . . Now imagine that you become your dreams and see what they reply . . . Tell your dreams what help you would like from them . . . Now become your dreams again and see what they reply . . . Become yourself again and tell your dreams that you are going to leave them soon for the time being, but that you will be staying in touch with them ... See what your dreams reply, and if they have anything else to say to you . . . Carry on this dialogue for a moment or two . . . You are going to take your leave now, although it's only a temporary leave, but before you go, ask your dreams for a sign or symbol to remember them by . . . When you have received this take your leave of your dreams . . . You begin to feel your cloud is starting to float you away again, on beyond your dreams and out of your dream world . . . Now you are aware that you are beginning to drift gently downwards still carrying your dream symbol . . . Now as you continue to drift downwards you are aware of coming back into the room ... As your body touches the floor your cloud fades away . . . Now you can feel your body firmly on the floor . . . Slowly and in your own time, and still feeling relaxed, stretch, come fully back into the room, open your eyes and sit up.

At this point group members are asked not to start chatting but to take some paper and crayons and to draw their dream symbol. After this the group members who would like to, show their drawings to the group. Feedback and sharing at this point is requested in the form of brief statements. Discussions are discouraged at this point.

Summary

Some suggestions are presented for structuring group feedback and advice is provided for the therapist to manage dreamwork in a group. Three group techniques are presented: 'If this were my dream', psychodrama and sculpting. These are followed by some methods for creative dream group exercises and artwork.

9

Themes and Practical Issues in Dreamwork

This chapter covers some practical issues that are helpful to consider when working with clients' dreams. These include presenting dreamwork to the client, how to help the client remember and record dreams, and advice on the choice of method and dream. The chapter also discusses working with the dreams of bereaved clients as well as with other dreams of death.

Introducing the client to dreamwork

Once clients know that their therapist is interested in their dreams, they will usually bring more. Some colleagues report that none of their clients bring dreams to therapy. It is likely that therapists, as much as anyone else, hear selectively. So they will hear and pick up from the client material that fits into their own conceptual framework. Their clients will know this too and, if they mention a dream but their therapist does not respond to it, they will probably not bring more dreams to therapy even if they have them. Therefore, clients are shaped up fairly rapidly by their therapists' interests and inclinations, therefore if therapists are interested in dreams they need to make it clear to their clients, maybe by asking about dreams in their initial assessment. In order to encourage clients to bring dreams to therapy, therapists need to educate their clients about the importance of dreams, as well as normalizing them and giving clients permission to work with their dreams. Essentially, clients need to know that everybody dreams, and that our dreams, like our thoughts and feelings, have personal meanings for us.

The orientation and approach to working with dreams outlined in this book is integrative. While full coverage may not have been given to certain theoretical viewpoints, the strength of this approach is that many of the techniques presented can be used by therapists from very different orientations. Therapists will be able to adapt and incorporate the methods into their own particular styles and orientations.

It is usually most helpful to work with a recent dream, since the issues are still present in the client's mind. The premise is that the dream contains a message to the dreamer about their current psychological state and so it is more helpful to work with recent material. It is certainly not helpful to work on dreams that clients feel they have already worked out, therefore it is worth checking that the client hasn't got a satisfactory solution already. However, it is also true that old dreams, perhaps from childhood, and possibly nightmares or recurring dreams, may be important. In this case it is likely that, if the person remembers the dream or re-dreams it in the case of recurring dreams, then the old issue or feeling may be being repeated in the present. It is usually the case that once a recurring dream has been satisfactorily worked with, it is unlikely to recur.

Remembering and recording dreams

Sometimes the reasons that clients don't bring their dreams to therapy are related to resistances and anxieties which can be reflected in the lack of dream recall. It often happens that clients and people who attend workshops are able to remember little or nothing of their dreams. It can also happen that, in ongoing therapy, people who previously had good recall find they no longer remember their dreams. The following are some considerations when attempting to help people improve dream recall:

1   Since we all dream regularly, therapists need to make clear that the major issue is not absence of dreams, but absence of dream recall. Also, since each of us dream for between 500 and 1000 hours every year, it is impossible to expect total recall.

2   Clients need to be reminded that working with dreams can be a time-consuming occupation. Dreams are quickly forgotten unless time can be devoted to remembering and recording them. To a large extent, dream recall is a learned skill. The more we value our dreams and the more time we devote to working with them, the more we will remember them. Both motivation and practice are important.

3   With the exception of a few very vivid or recurring dreams, the only time to recall a dream is immediately upon waking from it. Occasionally, an event of the day will 'break' a dream, although unless this is 'fixed' in the memory in some way, this memory too is likely to be short-lived. Frequently, the 'mood' or 'emotional' content of the dream will linger on throughout the day. But unless an effort has been made to recall the actual content, it may not be possible to relate the mood to the actual dream.

4   Another common reason why some people don't remember their dreams is one of attitude. With some notable exceptions, dreams have a discredited role in modern Western society and we simply do not attach any importance to them. Basically, many people do not take their dreams seriously; they may be afraid of being laughed at, or

of boring others, if they recount their dreams. Alternatively, the discussion of dreams may not fit in with their personal image, especially if this is a 'macho' one. Some people associate dreams with the 'occult' and predictions and prophecies, while others will consider dreams the province of psychoanalysis, and so possibly connected with psychological disturbance. In view of all these factors, it is perhaps not surprising that many people do not give a great deal of credence or importance to remembering dreams. In all these cases a basic attitude change is required.

As there are such a variety of dreamwork techniques available, the good news is that it is possible to work creatively and therapeutically with even the most minute scrap of dream material, such as a single image or a feeling. It is possible for therapists to find a method of working with dream material that will suit their client's needs as well as their own inclinations and orientations. There are many hints to be found in the literature for dream recall. The steps given below have been put together on the basis that they are practical for average people with reasonably busy daily lives who are not prepared to spend an inordinate amount of time working with their dreams. These steps are directed at the dreamer, and therapists might prepare a handout for their clients that they can then talk through together, answering queries and suggesting individual variations where necessary.

Basic hints for recalling and recording your dreams

1 First make the decision that you are really interested in your dreams and want to remember them.
2 Decide by which method you will record your dreams: with a note book, pencil and torch, or with a tape recorder. Place everything ready next to your bed so that you can use it easily without having to get out of bed or move around much. Have the note book open at the correct page, or the recorder set in the position ready to record. It is helpful to head your page or tape with the date before you go to sleep.
3 Focus your attention on remembering and understanding your dreams before going to sleep by your own preferred method of 'dream incubation', such as relaxing, thinking about a topic on which you want clarification and so on.
4 If you wake during the night with a dream memory, write it down exactly as it happened – do not try to interpret it. It is possible that a few key words and images may be enough to stimulate a much fuller recollection of the dream in the morning. However, this does not work for everyone, and you may need to write down the dream verbatim.
5 When you wake in the morning, lie still and try to recall your dream before moving about and getting up. Sometimes it is easier to start with the end of the dream and work backwards. If you cannot recall the dream, try shifting your body back into the position in which you were sleeping. Often this action will

(Continued)

(Continued)

trigger a dream memory. Don't worry if you think you have forgotten parts of it, just write down what you can.

6 Make sure to record your dreams while still in bed, or immediately after getting up, but before becoming engaged in daytime activities. Very few dream memories will survive beyond this period unless you have made a conscious effort to remember them.

7 Transcribe your dream into your dream diary or journal as soon as possible. Write the account of the dream in the present tense and relate the dream to any landmarks of the previous day, including TV programmes, films, books, conversations and so on. Date the dream and give it a title that sums up, in a phrase, the theme of the dream.

8 If you understand the dream sufficiently at this stage, make a decision to follow up the dream with some action in your waking life.

It is worth pointing out that clients can try too hard to remember their dreams. The author's experience is that, if clients tell themselves that they must remember their dreams, they are often unlikely to do so. A more relaxed, permissive approach is more fruitful. There may also be psychological resistances to dream recall and the therapist may need to pay attention to these in therapy. For example, a client may be frightened of the disturbing images that they may recall, or that they may reveal too much of themselves to the therapist. It is also possible that transference issues such as wishing to please the therapist, or more likely the reverse, may impede dream recall. Often gentle exploration with the client, or simply some mental preparation, can produce effective results. Although the steps outlined above may be sufficient, there are a number of ways that the therapist can assist and encourage dream recall, and four of these are outlined below.

Dream incubation

The ancient practice of dream incubation was discussed in Chapter 1. In essence, the therapist might suggest that the client should go to bed in as relaxed and composed a manner as possible. The ritual of a 'pampered' bedtime routine will enhance the notion of activities associated with sleep as important and pleasant. The therapist can tell the client that, while in bed before sleeping, they might relax and let their mind dwell on the idea of dreaming, as well as making mental resolutions to recall their dreams.

Gestalt 'hot-seat' work

Steps for using this approach have been described in Chapter 5. It can also be used in therapy as another means of working with blockages to dream recall. The would-be dream-recallers might talk to their 'dreams', which they place, collectively, on the 'hot-seat'. This enables them to explore the nature of their resistances.

EXAMPLE

Moira was having difficulties recalling her dreams. The therapist, Robyn, suggested that she might explore this by placing her 'dreams' on the hot-seat:

Moira: Dreams – why can't I remember you? I'm sure that you are there and I would like to remember you. I want to know what you can show me about myself. But you don't come to me. You won't let me remember you.

Dreams: Yes, you are quite right. We are here. You can remember us if you want to.

Moira: I *do* want to, but you won't let me.

Dreams: To be honest Moira, we don't think you want to remember us.

This type of dialogue continued for a little while. Then Robyn made a suggestion to Moira:

Robyn: Perhaps you would like to ask your dreams what would happen if you did remember them?

Moira: OK, dreams. Maybe it is my fault that I don't remember you. But I think you know why, and I want you to tell me the reason.

Dreams: You are scared. You don't really want to find out what we have to show you about yourself [*pause*] You are really pretty satisfied with yourself as you are. You probably think that if you recognized what we had to show you, you might have to start making changes, and that would be too painful.

Moira: Well, it is true that there are painful things about myself that I don't really want to have to think about and to change. But perhaps you could help me, dreams?

Dreams: We think we can. If you could be a little less scared we could show you good things as well as painful things, and we could even show you how to make some changes.

Moira: That sounds more interesting and a bit less scary. If I start to trust you more, will you help me?

(Continued)

(Continued)

> *Dreams:* Yes – we'll do our best to help. But you have to acknowledge us.
>
> *Moira:* OK. I'll do my best to remember you and recognize your existence.

The learning of this piece of work was evident to Moira and Robyn did not labour it at this point in the therapy session. However, at the next session Moira laughingly admitted that she had recalled a dream. The theme of Moira's dream was her feeling that her mother was basically untrustworthy. This theme was fruitfully worked on in therapy.

Free-association exercise

Another exercise that therapists might suggest is one that clients can either carry out on their own as 'homework', or do in the therapy session. The therapist suggests that the client relaxes and silently says to themselves 'I don't remember my dreams because . . .' and finishes the sentence with whatever comes into their mind. The client continues until no more thoughts come into their mind. The client then says to themselves 'I do want to remember my dreams because . . .' and again finishes the sentence with what thoughts come into their mind. The client might then write down what they had remembered and bring it back to the next therapy session. If the exercise is carried out in the session, the client is encouraged to verbalize their thoughts.

Dream diaries

For those clients who wish to devote more time to developing their dream-work, both in and out of the therapy session, the therapist should encourage the keeping of dream diaries. A loose-leaf folder or a large note book, or a journal, can be used for this purpose. Alternate sheets of lined and unlined paper is a good format, enabling the dream to be written on the lined sheets and the work, notes, drawings and so on to be developed on the unlined sheets. The therapist can suggest a dream diary format as follows:

1 *A basic account of the dream:* note form will suffice. Notes of main symbols, dream action, themes and associated emotions are also helpful.
2 *The date:* this is essential for any study, comparisons, or retrospective sense to be made of the dream.
3 *A title, and a theme, of not more than one or two lines:* by the time a number of dream records have been accumulated the dreamer will not wish to read through all of them on a regular basis. The title and theme will provide a useful aid for recall and will help to highlight processes and changes in dream and waking life.
4 *Day residue:* a few notes of some of the significant or relevant aspects of the previous day will assist in dream interpretation. It will also help later to shed irrelevant material (day's dross) and throw light on some of the dream symbols.

The above should be recorded immediately, preferably upon waking, but in any event not later than the day following the dream.

When the client first begins to work with their dreams, they will need considerable help and encouragement from the therapist. However, as the client gets more skilled, they can carry out much of the work on their own. The therapist can suggest that the client may take the following steps at their leisure and at home as they become more skilled. Initially, it will probably be necessary for therapist and client to work on the dreams together during therapy.

1   The client may keep a dictionary of their own key dream symbols, which may be written or drawn. The meanings can be ascribed as the client comes to understand them. It is important for the client to keep a record of (a) changes in the symbol itself and (b) changes in the meaning of symbols.
2   The client should note a basic account of the behaviour and actions of the dream ego (usually the dreamer). The following three questions can be answered for each dream (brief notes or lists can be made):
    a   What is the ego doing or not doing in the dream?
    b   Is the dream ego active or passive?
    c   What is the dream ego feeling?
3   The client can note bizarre, unusual, powerful, mysterious, frightening or enjoyable aspects of the dream. These can be listed and one or two associations made for each.
4   The client can note any other relevant aspect; for example, conflicts, resolutions, dream enemies or dream friends.
5   The client may consider what the dream is telling them. At this stage it may be possible for the client to have made a complete or partial 'interpretation' of the dream. Any unresolved issues can then be discussed in the therapy session.
6   The client may wish to consider how they can 'actualize' the dream. The therapist might suggest that the client make a resolution of some kind, based on what they have learned from the dream, which they can put into action in their waking life.
7   Finally, it is useful for the client to highlight unresolved aspects of the dream, which they can return to on future occasions or discuss in therapy.

Keeping a dream diary enhances the empowering process of therapy, enabling and encouraging the client to become more self-sufficient and less reliant on the therapy relationship.

Another factor that inhibits dream recall and use is fear about the nature and content of dreams. The most common fear raised concerns of fear of death, and the next section of the chapter discusses dreams of death as well as working with the dreams of those who have been bereaved.

Bereavement, death and dreaming

Dreams of death

A common fear concerns a dream where the death of the dreamer, or of another, actually happens or is anticipated. The fact is that it is very common to dream of death, but very rare for an actual death to follow a dream death. Where a death does occur following a dream, the dreamer often reports some actual knowledge or half-processed information that such a death was likely. For example, the death may be of a sick or elderly relative, who was known to be ailing and failing, or about whom thoughts or fears of death may have been in the mind of the dreamer. It is possible that the dreamer may have noticed something about that person which at some point triggered a recognition that they were not in good health. It is fairly common for mothers to have dreams about the death of, or danger to, their children. At some, possibly unconscious, level a mother's worst fear is commonly of losing her child.

Occasionally the report is of a totally unexpected death that did occur in circumstances predicted in the dream, and shortly after the dream. In the absence of any more detailed evidence, the therapist should accept the dreamer's account. In one case, discussed at a workshop, someone reported a dream which had predicted her friend's death in a road accident. On closer examination it appeared that the friend had died while a passenger in a tragic motorway pile-up. The dream had involved the dreamer herself being injured when a bus mounted the pavement. There is a natural desire to make sense of our dreams and the two events in this example probably became linked in the dreamer's mind. Where dreamers dream of their own death, it's clear that death does not follow in 100 per cent of the cases – at least up to the time of reporting the dream!

In terms of the particular meaning or significance of dreams of death, in many cases the metaphorical significance of death provides the most satisfactory explanation. This has been discussed in Chapter 3. Death is often found to symbolize the end of one phase or aspect of the dreamer's life; usually such dreams can also be seen to indicate the beginning of something new.

> Renée is a French woman in her early twenties. She reported being very frightened about a dream of the death of her parents, who were still living in France. Work with the dream highlighted aspects of a fairly recent relationship with an Englishman to whom Renée was becoming committed. This commitment involved, for Renée, a decision to settle in England, although her original intention had been to return to France. The dream death of her parents reflected Renée's anxiety about leaving her parental country, as well as an acknowledgement that she was no longer emotionally dependent on her parents.

Dreams where the dreamer kills or otherwise harms others can also cause anxiety to many clients. While the dream may reflect unconscious or repressed feelings of hate, it is often the case that educating people about the dramatization aspect of dreams, and giving permission for the expression of hitherto unacceptable feelings, usually resolves the dream, particularly where this is recurring. In Chapter 3, Helena's dream of lobbing grenades onto her partner, who was subsequently killed in the dream, was discussed. Helena was able to interpret this satisfactorily in terms of her hitherto unresolved dispute with her partner. Acknowledgement of the dream enabled Helena to deal with her angry feelings. The authors have found no evidence that dreaming of death symbolizes an unacknowledged death wish. Clients have found many varied and fruitful ways of interpreting dream deaths, and have allayed their fears connected with them.

In terms of the fears that clients bring to dreamwork, people seem to feel most frightened about the idea of some external (occult) power, or a repressed part of the self, behaving in a destructive way towards the individual or persona (conscious self). What is often missed is the actual healing power contained within the psyche, and expressed through the dream. Contained within the distressing aspects of dreams lie the seeds for growth and reconciliation.

Bereavement dreams

People who have lost someone close to them may often have powerful dreams. These dreams can track the grieving process in all its stages of numbness, disorganization and reorganization. Dreams of people we have lost can come prior to death, as a form of anticipatory grief, shortly after the death or for many years afterwards. Working sensitively with these dreams can help the dreamer to work through the tasks of mourning and greatly assist the mourning process (Garfield, 1996).

Ancient folklore held that dreams were visitations from the dead who remained in communication with us. Kubler-Ross (1975) believed that dreams offer spiritual solace to those who have been bereaved. Whatever their personal belief system, therapists need to be particularly sensitive to the spiritual needs and beliefs of their clients in this area of working with dreams. It is not necessary to hold any particular belief to be sensitive to the needs of the client. Our dreams may speak to us and give us messages and, in a sense, it does not matter whether the client believes that the voice in their dreams comes from God, their departed loved one speaking to them, or their own inner voice. It is still possible to work with the dream and its message in many of the same ways that have been described in the book.

The following example is a dream gifted by a colleague whose husband had died 18 months previously. Her description of the dream and her reflections on it are presented verbatim.

EXAMPLE

Dreaming of Hazz

Context for the dream

At the time of my dream I was feeling particularly alone and, with the exception of my young son, on the outside of all relationships with no sense of belonging.

(Continued)

(Continued)

The Dream

In my dream I wake to find that I'm lying in bed beside Hazz. It's the bedroom of the house that we lived in for 23 years, there's nothing in the room but the bed and us. I know Hazz is dead but his body is still warm and it's nice lying beside him in the bed, and room, we shared together for so many years. The colours of the room are creamy and soft. I know I must get up and get ready for work and, at the same time, I know I must do something about Hazz, he is dead after all and surely will start to decompose. But there's time, I know I'll sort it, but how and when isn't clear yet. I don't know if I tried to move Hazz or how it happened but when I get out of bed he is lying across it from side to side. I carry on, get dressed and go out, but as I'm driving to work it suddenly dawns on me that the cleaner is coming and may be alarmed to find Hazz in the bed, so I hurry back. It's too late, the cleaner has been and gone and somehow managed to move Hazz to the top of the stairwell wall. I can see him up there but I can't reach him, can't work out what to do and worry about how I'll be able to make the necessary arrangements. I wake from the dream feeling perplexed.

Although I remembered the dream very clearly I didn't make any attempts to interpret it beyond the apparent meaning, i.e. a need to put Hazz 'to rest' and move on. Instead, I held the dream until I could discuss it with Delia.

Talking to Delia

Talking the dream through with Delia enabled me to recognize new dimensions to the dream. In particular the idea that, despite his death, Hazz was still able to provide me with a feeling of comfort but it was only when others, i.e. the 'cleaner', became involved that this quality was disturbed. This paralleled my lived experience around the time of his illness and death, i.e. when it was just the two of us things were fine; however, when others involved themselves matters became complicated, and these complications clouded the relationship between us. So if I were to put Hazz 'to rest', then what I really needed to do was clear the way between us and reclaim the positive parts of our history.

Since then I have begun to create a journal of each of the 33 years that we spent together. This has brought to the surface the many things we did together, music we listened to and the friends we spent time with. It has given me a sense of reclaiming our life together, good and bad, but also the parts of myself that existed during my life with him.

In this example no particular method was used, although some of the questions described earlier in the chapter in the section on dream diaries were helpful. This is a particularly nice example of 'actualizing' the dream; that is, making a dream product that takes the dreamer forward in waking life. This can be especially helpful in working with bereaved dreamers since it helps the dreamer remember the person whom they've lost.

The next two dreams were also given by a colleague, Carol, who has, in recent years, lost a best friend but has also very recently lost her mother and father within a few weeks of each other.

EXAMPLE

Dreaming of Val

Context for the dream

I had this dream during the particularly difficult months nursing my father in his final illness and visiting my mother in hospital. I missed Val a lot, particularly the opportunities to get out and 'play' with her. Years ago Val's mother had been in the same hospital as my mother, and Val had been glad of my support. I'd always expected that she would be there for me when I faced the end of my parents' lives.

Just before my father became ill I had gone on a march against cuts. I thought of Val a lot as she and I had been on many marches over the years. The last one we went on together was the march against the Iraq War. She died three years ago last April.

Dream

It's a nice warm spring or summer day and Val and I are out walking on a country lane. We come across a large house and it seems as if it might be National Trust, so we go in. We hadn't planned this but the house looks interesting and we start to go round it. There seems to be some sort of function on with drinks and food and we help ourselves to some.

Someone (a posh woman, I think) comes and tells us in an officious way that there is a private function and we aren't allowed to stay, and then they go off. Val says 'Blow that, we haven't had a good look round yet and we aren't doing any harm.' I feel a bit anxious and think we'll get into trouble if we get caught, but with Val there I feel safe enough to take the chance. We have a good look round and have a laugh. There's a feeling of standing up to the upper-classes.

When we get outside we notice that the house is not made of stone or brick but is a bit like a gingerbread house but made out of wickerwork. We both think this is strange and we didn't notice it when we went in. I feel I've had a mini adventure and really appreciate Val's company and encouragement to break some rules.

This dream could be seen in at least two ways, either as anticipatory grief for the dreamer's father or as a grieving dream for Carol's close friend, Val, or maybe both. It is often the case that one impending loss can trigger memories of an earlier. Carol's next dream occurred soon after the death of her father.

EXAMPLE

Dreaming of Dad

Context for the dream

I'm on a solitary holiday in Wales just after my father's funeral and I'm walking on the Gower. Although it's July it isn't very warm, but it's dry and pleasant for walking. I'm feeling quite at peace and a degree of relief that the awful illnesses are over and my parents have died within five weeks of each other.

Dream

I've been walking on coastal paths but today decide to walk inland and I've worked out a circular walk through woods and fields. Somehow I find I'm lost and begin to feel distressed, tearful and a bit scared. I'm feeling much younger and I want my Dad. Out loud I talk to him and ask him to help me find my way. I'm afraid I might have strayed into the private estate nearby and I'll be in trouble with a gamekeeper or there might be a wild bull. Everything is lush because it's high summer and in places it's boggy underfoot. I start to feel tired. Then I spot a way mark and a stile and get back on to the path. I feel relief and thank my Dad but also wonder how long he will stay around to help me find my way if I get lost again.

This dream is a good example of the dreamer feeling that her father has returned in her dream to help her. Sometimes it can be comforting to remind bereaved clients that those they have lost remain with them in their thoughts and memories as well as in their dreams.

It might have been possible for the dreams of my colleagues to have been worked on further, since they have rich symbols and imagery. However, the dreamers in these cases had no wish or need to do this, they felt pleased and empowered by the work described. It is important to remember that the dream is interpreted when it makes sense to the dreamer.

Summary

Ideas for introducing the client to dreamwork are followed by tips for remembering and recording dreams. There are also exercises for helping clients who wish to remember their dreams but who have little recall. The next section of the chapter concerns working with dreams of death and there are some suggestions for working with clients who are disturbed by death occurring in a dream. The final section contains some examples of working with the dreams of clients who have been bereaved.

Conclusion

These bereavement dreams conclude the book, which has been about the importance of dreams in the therapy process. A variety of ideas and methods have been presented which will give therapists the confidence to facilitate dreamwork with their clients. The book is written from an integrative perspective and therapists from a variety of orientations should find it helpful. Underlying all the approaches is the premise that dreams belong to the dreamer and that only they can satisfactorily interpret their dreams. One role of the therapist is to stimulate the client's interest to incorporate their dreams into their waking life in their own way. Therefore it is suggested to therapists that dreamwork is a powerful and collaborative therapeutic tool, which can lead the client away from dependency towards empowerment. Readers are encouraged to develop the interest and confidence to explore their dreams and those of their clients and to discover new and creative ways of working with them.

References

American Academy of Sleep Medicine, European Sleep Research Society, the Japanese Society of Sleep Research & the Latin American Sleep Society (2001). *International Classification of Sleep Disorders*. Westchester, IL: American Academy of Sleep Medicine.

American Psychiatric Association (2004). *Diagnostic and Statistical Manual of Mental Disorders* (4th ed., text revision). Washington, DC: American Psychiatric Association.

Aserinsky, E., & Kleitman, N. (1953). Regularly occurring periods of eye mobility and concomitant phenomena during sleep. *Science*, 118: 273.

Barrett, D. (2004). The 'Royal Road' becomes a shrewd shortcut: The use of dreams in focused treatment. In R. L. Rosner, W. J. Lyddon, & A. Freeman (Eds). *Cognitive Therapy and Dreams*. New York: Springer.

Beck, A. T. (1971). Cognitive patterns in dreams and daydreams. In J. H. Masserman (Ed). *Dream Dynamics: Science and Psychoanalysis* (pp. 2–7). New York: Grune & Stratton.

Beck, A. T., Rush, A. J., Shaw, B. E., & Emery, G. (1979). *Cognitive Therapy of Depression*. New York: Guilford Press.

Beck, A. T., & Ward, C. H. (1961). Dreams of depressed patients: Characteristic themes in manifest content. *Archives of General Psychiatry*, 5, 462–467.

Beck, J. S. (1995). *Cognitive Therapy: Basics and Beyond*. New York: Guilford Press.

Berne, E. (1964). *Games People Play*. New York: Ballantine.

Blagrove, M. (2007). Dreaming and personality. In D. Barrett, & P. McNamara (Eds). *The New Science of Dreaming: Vol 2. Content, Recall, and Personality Correlates*. Westport, CT: Paeger.

Blagrove, M. (2009). Dreaming – motivated or meaningless? *The Psychologist*, 22, 680–683.

Blatner, A. (1973). *Acting In – Practical Applications of Psychodramatic Methods*. New York: Springer.

Chetwynd, T. (1974). *Dictionary for Dreamers*. London: Paladin.

Clarkson, P. (2004). *Gestalt Counselling in Action*. London: Sage.

Cushway, D. (2010). Reflective practice and humanistic psychology: The whole is more than the sum of the parts. In J. Stedman, & R. Dallos (Eds). *Reflective Practice in Psychotherapy and Counselling.* Maidenhead: Open University Press.

Davis, J. L. (2009). *Treating Post-Trauma Nightmares.* New York: Springer.

Davis, J. L., Byrd, P., Rhudy, J. L., & Wright, D. C. (2007). Characteristics of chronic nightmares in a trauma-exposed treatment-seeking sample. *Dreaming, 17,* 187–198.

Domhoff, G. W. (2003). *The Scientific Study of Dreams: Neural Networks, Cognitive Development, and Content Analysis.* Washington, DC: American Psychological Association.

Dowd, E. T. (2004). Foreward. In R. L. Rosner, W. J. Lyddon, & A. Freeman (Eds). *Cognitive Therapy and Dreams.* New York: Springer.

Doweiko, H. E. (1982). Neurobiology and dream theory: A rapprochement model. *Individual Psychology: The Journal of Adlerian Theory, Research and Practice, 38,* (1), 55–61.

Doweiko, H. E. (2004). In R. L. Rosner, W. J. Lyddon, & A. Freeman (Eds). *Cognitive Therapy and Dreams.* New York: Springer.

Duke, L. A., Allen, D. N., Rozee, P. D., & Bommaritto, M. (2007). The sensitivity and specificity of flashbacks and nightmares in trauma. *Anxiety Disorders, 22,* 319–327.

Ernst, S., & Goodison, L. (1981). *In Our Own Hands: Book of Self-help Therapy.* London: Women's Press.

Faraday, A. (1972). *Dream Power.* New York: Berkeley.

Faraday, A. (1974). *The Dream Game.* New York: Harper & Rowe.

Flanagan, O. (2000). *Dreaming Souls.* Oxford: Oxford University Press.

Foa, E. B., Keane, T. M., & Friedman, M. J. (2000). *Effective Treatments for PTSD.* New York: Guilford Press.

Freeman, A., & White, B. (2002). Dreams and the dream image: Using dreams in cognitive therapy. *Journal of Cognitive Psychotherapy: An International Quarterly, 16,* 174–177.

Freeman, A., & White, B. (2004). Dreams and the dream image: Using dreams in cognitive therapy. In R. L. Rosner, W. J. Lyddon, & A. Freeman (Eds). *Cognitive Therapy and Dreams.* New York: Springer.

Freud, S. (1900/1976). *The Interpretation of Dreams.* Harmondsworth: Penguin.

Garfield, P. L. (1974). *Creative Dreaming.* New York: Ballantine.

Garfield, P. L. (1984). *Your Child's Dreams.* New York: Ballantine.

Garfield, P. L. (1986). Nightmares in sexually abused female teenagers. Paper presented at the meeting of the Association for the Study of Dreams, Ottawa, Canada.

Garfield, P. L. (1996). Dreams in bereavement. In D. Barrett (Ed). *Trauma and Dreams.* Cambridge, MA: Harvard University Press.

Germain, A., Krakow, B., Faucher, B., Zadra, A., Nielsen, T., Hollifield, M., Warner, T. D., & Kos, M. (2004). Increased mastery elements associated with imagery rehearsal treatment for nightmares in sexual assault survivors with PTSD. *Dreaming, 14,* 195–206.

Germain, A., & Nielson, T. A. (2003). Sleep pathophysiology in posttraumatic stress disorder and idiopathic nightmare sufferers. *Biological Psychiatry, 54,* 1092–1098.

Green, C. (1968). *Lucid Dreams.* Oxford: Institute for Psychophysical Research.

Hackmann, A., Bennett-Levy, J., & Holmes, E. A. (2011). *Oxford Guide to Imagery in Cognitive Therapy.* Oxford: Oxford University Press.

Halliday, G. (1987). Direct psychological therapies for nightmares: A review. *Clinical Psychology Review, 7,* 501–523.

Hamzelou, J. (2010). The secret of consciousness: Reinterpreting dreams. *New Scientist, 206,* 36–39.

Hartmann, E. (1984). *The Nightmare.* New York: Basic Books.

Hearne, K. (1990). *The Dream Machine.* Wellingborough: Aquarian Press.

Hill, C. E. (1996). Working with dreams in psychotherapy. New York: Guilford Press.

Hill, C. E. (2004). *Dream Work in Therapy: Facilitating Exploration, Insight and Action.* Washington, DC: The American Psychological Association.

Hill, C. E., & Rochlen, A. B. (2004). The Hill Cognitive-Experiential model of dream interpretation. In R. L. Rosner, W. J. Lyddon, & A. Freeman (Eds). *Cognitive Therapy and Dreams.* New York: Springer.

Hobson, J.A., & McCarley, R.W. (1977). The brain as a dream state generator: An activation-synthesis hypothesis of the dream process. *American Journal of Psychiatry, 134,* 1335–1348.

Houston, G. (2003). *Brief Gestalt Therapy.* London: Sage.

Joyce, P., & Sills, C. (2010). *Skills in Gestalt Counselling and Psychotherapy.* London: Sage.

Jung, C. G. (1978). *Man and his Symbols.* London: Picador.

Jung, C. G. (2002). *Dreams.* London: Routledge.

Kaplan Williams, S. (1984). *The Dreamwork Manual.* Wellingborough: Aquarian Press.

Karp, M., Holmes, P., & Bradshaw, K. (Eds) (1998). *The Handbook of Psychodrama.* London: Routledge.

Kellner, R., Neidhardt, J., Krakow, B., & Pathak, D. (1992). Changes in chronic nightmares after one session of desensitisation or rehearsal instructions. *American Journal of Psychiatry, 149,* 659–663.

Krakow, B. (2004). Imagery rehearsal therapy for chronic posttraumatic nightmares: A minds eye view. In R. L. Rosner, W. J. Lyddon, & A. Freeman (Eds). *Cognitive Therapy and Dreams.* New York: Springer.

Krakow, B., & Zadra, A. (2006). Clinical management of chronic nightmares: Imagery rehearsal therapy. *Behavioral Sleep Medicine, 4,* 45–70.

Kramer, M. (2007). *The Dream Experience: A Systematic Exploration.* New York: Routledge.

Kubler-Ross, E. (1975). *Death: The Final Stage of Growth.* New York: Prentice Hall.

La Berge, S. (1985). *Lucid Dreaming.* New York: Ballantine.

La Berge, S. (2004). *Lucid Dreaming: A Concise Guide to Awakening in Your Dreams.* Boulder, CO: Sounds True.

Leveton, E. (2001). *A Clinician's Guide to Psychodrama*. New York: Springer.

Moreno, J. L. (1987). In J. Fox (Ed). *The Essential Moreno*. New York: Springer.

Neimeyer, R. A., & Stewart, A. E. (2000). Constructivist and narrative psychotherapies. In C. R. Snyder, & R. E. Ingram (Eds). *Handbook of Psychological Change: Psychotherapy Processes and Practices for the 21st Century* (pp. 217–242). New York: Wiley.

Neylan, T. C., Marmar, C. R., Metzler, T. J., Weiss, D. S., Zatzick, D. F., Delucchi, K. L., & Schoenfeld, F. B. (1998). Sleep disturbances in the Vietnam generation: Findings from a nationally representative sample of male Vietnam veterans. *American Journal of Psychiatry, 155*, 929–933.

Nielson, T. A., Kuiken, D., & Alain, G. (2004). Immediate and delayed incorporations of events into dreams. *Journal of Sleep Research, 13*, 327–336.

Nielson, T. A., & Stenstrom, P. (2005). What are the memory sources of dreaming? *Nature, 437*, 1286–1289.

Ohayon, M. M., & Shapiro, C. M. (2000). Sleep disturbance and psychiatric disorders associated with post-traumatic stress disorder in the general population. *Comprehensive Psychia\try, 41*, 469–478.

Pagel, J. F., & Parnes, B. L. (2001). Medications for the treatment of sleep disorders: An overview. *Primary Care Companion Journal of Clinical Psychiatry, 3*, 118–125.

Revonuso, A. (2000). The reinterpretation of dreams. *Behavioural and Brain Sciences, 23*, 877–901.

Rosner, R. L., Lyddon, W. J., & Freeman, A. (Eds) (2004). *Cognitive Therapy and Dreams*. New York: Springer.

Royal College of Psychiatrists (2010). *Post-traumatic Stress Disorder*. London: Royal College of Psychiatrists.

Rycroft, C. (1981). *The Innocence of Dreams*. Oxford: Oxford University Press.

Sanford, J. A. (1968). *Dreams: God's Forgotten Language*. New York: Crossroad.

Shohet, R. (1985). *Dream Sharing*. Wellingborough: Turnstone.

Solms, M. (1997). *The Neuropsychology of Dreams*. Mahwah, NJ: Lawrence Erlbaum.

Stewart, K. (1969). 'Dream theory in Malaya'. In C. T. Tart (Ed), *Advanced States of Consciousness: A Book of Readings*. London: Wiley.

Stickgold, R., Hobson, J., Fosse, R., & Fosse, M. (2001). Sleep, learning and dreams. *Science, 294*, 1052–1057.

Taylor, J. (1983). *Dream Work*. New York: Paulist Press.

Ullman, M., & Zimmerman, N. (1983). *Working with Dreams*. London: Hutchinson.

Weiss, L. (1986). *Dream Analysis in Psychotherapy*. New York: Pergamon.

Wiseman, A. S. (1986). *Nightmare Help*. Berkeley, CA: Ten Speed Press.

Young, J. E. (1999). *Cognitive Therapy for Personality Disorders: A Schema-Focused Approach* (4th ed.). Sarasota, FL: Professional Resources Exchange.

Zayfert, C., & DeViva, J. C. (2004). Residual insomnia following cognitive behavioural therapy for PTSD. *Journal of Traumatic Stress, 17*, 69–73.

Index